POLITICS AIN'T BEANBAG*

*(WITH APOLOGIES TO FINLEY PETER DUNNE)

By

John C. Pittenger

authorHOUSE™

1663 LIBERTY DRIVE, SUITE 200
BLOOMINGTON, INDIANA 47403
(800) 839-8640
WWW.AUTHORHOUSE.COM

First published by AuthorHouse 08/31/05

ISBN: 1-4208-3797-4 (e)
ISBN: 1-4208-3796-6 (sc)

Library of Congress Control Number: 2005904944

Printed in the United States of America
Bloomington, Indiana

This book is printed on acid-free paper.

About the Title Page

Finley Peter Dunne was a newspaperman who between 1893 and 1919 wrote a series of columns in the Chicago Evening Post, later collected in eight volumes, which took the form of conversations between two imaginary Irishmen, Mr. Dooley(the bartender) and Mr. Henessey(the customer). They ranged over a wide variety of topics, but treated with wit and wisdom politicians ranging from Teddy Roosevelt ("Alone in Cubia") to the local ward heeler. Mr. Dooley's admonition to Mr. Henessey -- "politics ain't beanbag" -- seemed a fitting title for this small book about local and state politics a century later.

Dedication

To Pauline,
the light of my life these past twenty-five years.

Acknowledgements

I acknowledge with gratitude the assistance of a number of people in making this a better book than it would otherwise have been. At the same time I absolve them of any responsibility for errors which may have survived their scrutiny.

Among those who read all or parts of the manuscript and offered useful (if not always heeded) advice were Richard A. Doran, Rick Frankhouser, Peter Garland, John W. Hartman, Joseph Karlesky, John Kincaid, Christopher King, Peter Kuriloff, Stanley J. Michalak, G. Terry Madonna, Jerome Murphy, Joseph F. Roda, David P. Schuyler, John H. Vanderzell, Debra Weiner, Mark P. Widoff and Robert C. Wise.

I owe a special debt of thanks to two young people, Kelly Ferguson, who undertook the arduous task of deciphering my increasingly unreadable handwriting, and Eric Geiger, who helped with the tedious business of proofreading the galleys. For them, I hope that this is only the beginning of a life-long interest in politics and public affairs.

Preface

About ten years ago, as I approached the end of what an economist would call my useful (that is, my employable) life, I began to ponder what I had seen and done, and, especially, what I had learned in a half-life in politics.

So I began making notes about the various phases of what has proven to be a rather chequered career. I am an amateur at heart, not someone who has been willing to put political advancement at the very top of my agenda. But I enjoy the democratic process, and have bounced from one part of it to another, with interludes, both long and short, for teaching, deaning, coaching, writing, and other diversions.

At first these phases seemed largely unrelated to each other. But as I began thinking more systematically about the past 45 years, a pattern emerged; it took the form of a slow but steady metamorphosis from being an idealist, i.e., someone who thinks he can impose his version of Utopia on the rest of the human race, to a kind of pragmatism in which one takes into account the eternal cussedness of the human race, but thinks, nonetheless, that it is possible, at the very least, to stave off doomsday, and perhaps, even, to improve things a bit.

Henry Adams described himself as an Eighteenth Century man forced to cope with a radically uncongenial Nineteenth Century. The result, notwithstanding the fact that he was superbly qualified, in all except temperament, for public life, was a growing disenchantment with and disassociation from the world. My own dissonances, equally strong, led me in a different direction; whether from a sanguine temperament, or some other unknown cause, they forced me to reexamine my prejudices (as I later understood them to be) and allowed me to plunge into politics with enthusiasm if not with optimism.

So this little book is partly the tale of my political education. It should not have taken forty-five years, but it did; I guess I am a slow learner. Even now, it is incomplete. Though I understand, intellectually, that many of the premises from which I began in my twenties were mistaken, I have had a hard time emotionally embracing these conclusions, which accounts for much of my backsliding, as, for example, my foolhardy run for the United States Senate in 1980.

The other theme that emerges from a perusal of the past forty-five years is how much satisfaction I have derived from my various forays into public life, and how much they have contributed to the definition of who I am. It perturbs me to hear people denigrating politics and politicians. (Not long after my wife and I moved into our retirement community I overheard a trio of elderly ladies talking about me. "He's THE POLITICIAN," one said, with evident scorn. I wanted to say, "and proud of it," but dared not reveal that I had been eavesdropping.)

I have spent much of my adult life urging young people to become politically active, in whatever party and at whatever level of government they choose. I try to be honest with them about the pleasures and penalties of public life: you won't get rich (unless you are a crook); you will wield far less power than most citizens assume to be at the disposal of any public servant; and you will suffer the slings and arrows of a Fourth Estate more interested in entertaining than informing the citizenry. But you will have the great good fortune to be able to answer the challenge which Benjamin Franklin is supposed to have made to a society lady who, encountering Franklin in Philadelphia one hot day in the summer of 1787, asked, "And what have you given us, Dr. Franklin?" To which he is supposed to have replied, "A Republic, Madam – if you can keep it."

Having helped in a small way to "keep the Republic" is ample compensation for me, as I hope it will be to countless others.

Table of Contents

Chapter 1 - Beginnings

According to family lore, my interest in politics dates back at least to the age of five, when I am alleged to have stood on the wood basket in our living room and announced my intention of running for President. The story may be apocryphal; there is no one now alive who can confirm it. But there can be no doubt that I was smitten at an early age.

That is not surprising. Both my parents, though from widely differing backgrounds, had more than a passing interest in public life. My father, Nicholas O. Pittenger, was the ninth of twelve children of a blind itinerant Methodist preacher. He was thus a Hoosier, a Methodist and a Republican; and although he abandoned Methodism as a young man (a clear case, I think, of an overdose, his father and two brothers having been Methodist preachers), the attachment to Republicanism lasted a good deal longer. (He claimed to have thrown a rotten tomato at William Jennings Bryan, the arch enemy, in 1892, but like a good many of my father's tales, this one is suspect.)

My father seems to have made his own political debut in Bloomington, Indiana where, after graduating from the University in 1911, he became manager of the University bookstore. He served on the Bloomington City Council, having first been elected, according to another of his tales, by buying a wagonload of watermelons at a bargain price and distributing them in the poorer section of town.

In 1923, he migrated East to Swarthmore, Pennsylvania, having accepted the invitation of Frank Aydelotte, a fellow Hoosier and the newly appointed President of Swarthmore College, to become Controller of the college. Here his first wife, Bess Williams, died the following year, and here he married his second wife, my mother, Cornelia Vander Veer Chapman, in 1928. Picking up where he had left off, he served two terms on Borough Council in Swarthmore, put there largely, I suspect, to protect the college's interests. He had no interest in abstract ideas, but enjoyed people hugely. When not in his office (which was a surprising amount of the time) he could generally be found at Michael's Drug Store, smoking one of his cheap White Owl cigars and chewing things over with Mr. Michael and the other town fathers, or at the riding stables, where our three horses were quartered during the school year.

My mother's interest in politics was more theoretical. Her father, Elwood Chapman, came from an old but undistinguished family of Philadelphia Quakers whose progenitor had come to Pennsylvania in 1684. Grandpa Chapman worshipped at the shrine of Theodore Roosevelt; an immense portrait of TR hung over the roll-top desk in his study. His brother-in-law, Robert Stults, a composer of treacly popular ballads ("The Sweetest Story Ever Told") was, on the other hand, a fervent admirer of Woodrow Wilson. I remember hearing, as a child, about their political altercations at Sunday dinner, sometimes ending in most un-Quakerly behavior. Grandma Chapman, who hailed from a Dutch clan that settled in Long Branch, New Jersey, in the late 1600s, is not known to have expressed any political opinions whatsoever. Perhaps she thought that Elwood and Robert between them had enough for the whole family.

My mother was educated at the Friends Central School and at Swarthmore College, just across the railroad tracks from the house to which the Chapmans had moved in 1912. At Swarthmore she came under the influence of Professor Robert Brooks of the Political Science Department, a noted liberal and apparently a stimulating teacher. In 1932 she cast her vote not for Franklin Roosevelt, but for Norman Thomas, the Socialist candidate (she thought FDR too wishy washy). She later became, however, a staunch supporter of FDR and an active member of what was then a tiny Democratic community in the town.

The Spanish Civil War was an issue that greatly agitated the Swarthmore faculty during the late 1930s. President Aydelotte had been instrumental in helping a number of Jewish and other academics to escape from Nazi Germany and settle in the United States. Partly for that reason interest in European events ran high on campus; I remember my mother knitting caps and mittens for the Loyalist forces in Spain. But when I talked about all this at school I found that most of my classmates were quite oblivious.

The presidential election of 1940 was a traumatic event in our household. My mother was, of course, for FDR, having been converted by the New Deal. But my father had been a friend and fraternity brother of Wendell Willkie's at Indiana University. As a result, he became an honorary chairman of the Citizens for Willkie in Pennsylvania, although I don't remember him putting in much time on the campaign.

The climax, for me, came on a hot day in August of 1940 when my father decided to pay a call on "Wendell" at his headquarters in the old Benjamin Franklin Hotel at 8th and Chestnut Streets in Philadelphia. Balloting at the Republican Convention was to begin that very night. We were not making much headway getting past the security guards when one of Wendell's brothers spotted my father and led us to the candidate's lair. Willkie looked just like his pictures: hair in his eyes, tie askew, sweating profusely. He asked my father if we would be his guests at the Convention that night; to my horror, my father said, "No, I promised his mother I'd have him home by nine o'clock." So I missed out on a chance to see the great man nominated.

The ride back to the farm that evening was a long and silent one. When we arrived, I announced my conversion to the Republican Party, to which my mother replied, "then I guess you'll have to feed yourself." So I became a Democrat again, and have remained one ever since. We had no radio at the farm, or at least none that worked, so I went to the house across the dirt road to listen to the roll-call vote with our neighbors; but the static of summer thunderstorms made listening an ordeal, and I went to bed without knowing whether my father would be a good friend of the Republican candidate for President. And although my sister and I debated whether our parents would divorce, in fact there was no acrimony.

The 1944 presidential election was, from my perspective, far less exciting. I remember being one of the few supporters of FDR in my 10th grade homeroom, and little else. But the campaign contributed to my political education in one unanticipated way. Delaware County was then represented in Congress by an isolationist Republican Congressman named James Wolfenden. The Democrats drafted to run against him one Vernon O'Rourke, a handsome Irishman, a junior professor of political science at Swarthmore College then serving with the Navy in the Pacific Theatre. As he could not campaign for himself a large and enthusiastic group of faculty and students were recruited on his behalf.

One bright Saturday morning in early October my parents were persuaded to let me join a group of undergraduates who were going to leaflet Upper Darby, a very Republican town on the edge of Philadelphia. I was only 14, but tall for my age, so I was given the assignment of putting O'Rourke posters wherever they might attract some notice.

I was busy tacking posters on every available tree and telephone pole when an Upper Darby police officer sauntered up. "What are you doing, sonny," he asked in a not unkindly voice. I explained that I was putting up O'Rourke posters. "But it's illegal to put posters on utility company property – you'll have to take them down." I said, "OK, but I'm going to take down the Wolfenden posters too." "No, you can't do that, because I didn't see anyone put them up." At that point I gave him some lip, and was bustled off to the town jail, where my father bailed me out a couple of hours later. Moral: the law depends on who's enforcing it.

In the fall of 1945, my parents having retired to our farm in southern Chester County, I enrolled in the 11th grade at the Phillips Exeter Academy in Exeter, New Hampshire. My two years there were largely devoid of political activity. Arthur Schlesinger, Jr., who preceded me at Exeter by 14 years, notes in his autobiography that Exeter and Andover, highly competitive but rather secular schools, produced proportionately fewer public servants than church-related schools like Groton and St. Paul's. But my liberal convictions were strongly fortified by the teaching of Henry W. Bragdon, a nominal Eisenhower Republican but an ardent advocate of civil rights and a wonderfully stimulating teacher who became almost a foster-father to me.

I remember one episode, involving Governor Robert Bradford of Massachusetts, a Republican who gave a guest lecture and then met individually with interested students. When I described the Pennsylvania political scene, he said mournfully, "It must be wonderful to come from a state where not all the Catholics are Democrats and not all the Protestants are Republicans." In 1946 he was swept out of office on a tide of Catholic votes inspired by a ballot referendum on contraceptives, thus confirming his own worst fears.

At Harvard, in the fall of 1947, I ran unsuccessfully for Student Council. My defeat was a blessing in disguise, because it freed me to devote a very substantial part of my undergraduate years to

6

Phillips Brooks House, the center of Harvard and Radcliffe social work, leading a group of a dozen boys in Ward 22 in the Brighton section of Boston. That experience, including a summer as director of recreation in the same neighborhood, gave me some insight into the culture of a community very different from the one I had grown up in. My father and I had one of our rare quarrels about that summer job. His view, reflecting no doubt his own experience, was that any deserving youngster would make it out of poverty on his own and that by helping the undeserving poor I was simply interfering with the survival of the fittest. I didn't buy that theory then and I don't buy it now.

I don't remember campaigning for Truman at Harvard in the Fall of 1948, but I have one vivid recollection of that election. All of my roommates that year were Republicans. We stayed up listening to the radio until 2 a.m., when Dewey's election seemed assured; but I set the alarm for 6 a.m., just in time to learn that Ohio had swung into the Democratic column giving Truman the victory. I woke my roommates with the cheerful news; it's a wonder they didn't toss me out of the third floor Dunster House window.

The 1948 election was memorable for one other reason: my father's quite surprising conversion to the Democratic Party. In seeking to explain this to his Republican friends, he described himself as "worn down" by his wife and two children. My mother had a more interesting explanation. Sometime during 1948 the New Yorker published a brief essay called "The Governor's Corn." It seems that Governor Dewey and Lowell Thomas, the radio announcer, had adjoining estates in Pawling, New York. Each fall they would go out in the Governor's limousine to see who had grown the tallest stalk. My father was offended -- not, I think, by the contest itself, because he annually displayed his tallest corn stalks in the lobby of the Swarthmore National Bank – but by the limousine. That, plus his admiration for Harry Truman's pluck and common sense, meant that for the first time in 20 years of married life my parents' presidential votes did not cancel each other out.

As a senior at Harvard, I decided to write an undergraduate thesis which would naturally be about some aspect of politics. My tutor, Oscar Handlin, sent me down the Charles River to the Massachusetts Institute of Technology to talk to a young political scientist, John Morton Blum, who was doing some research on the election of 1912. Since he was interested in finding out what sorts of people had enlisted in TR's third party crusade, I agreed to write about TR and the Bull Moose Party in Pennsylvania. I enjoyed the interviews with elderly ward leaders, but the hours spent browsing through back numbers of the Philadelphia North American alongside the winos in the newspaper room of the Free Library of Philadelphia were tedious and helped me to decide, in the end, that a scholarly career was not my cup of tea.

My political education was both helped and hindered by the accident of my being awarded a Frank Knox Fellowship, recently established under the will of Franklin Roosevelt's wartime Secretary of the Navy. According to the terms of the fellowship, the recipient could study at any university in the British Commonwealth, the only stipulation being that one could not take any examinations or be working toward a degree. I knew I wanted to be in England - ten years of Gilbert and Sullivan had worked their magic - and chose the London School of Economics rather than Oxford or Cambridge in order to be at the center of things, politically speaking.

So I set sail for Europe on the Isle de France in early September of 1951 with my Harvard classmate, Tony Oettinger, who had won a fellowship to Cambridge. I soon found "digs" in the north of London with a very curious American family. Mr. Hallinan was an American Socialist who refused to register for the draft during World War I; as a result, he and his wife, Hazel Hunkins Hallinan, decamped for England where conscientious objectors were treated somewhat more leniently. He became a financial columnist; she, a devoted feminist and an ardent member of the left wing of the Labour Party. Each morning I could overhear Hazel discussing with her friends, Monica and Jessica, what those "bastards in the House of Commons" had done to some project or policy of the feminist movement.

The Hallinan household was the setting for one of the most hilarious episodes in my political education. Senator Hubert Humphrey had come to London to see how The Marshall Plan was working. Hazel, completely misreading the situation and equating the left wing of the Democratic Party with the left wing of the Labour Party, invited Humphrey to Sunday tea, along with several left-wing Labour members of Parliament. Humphrey arrived late. Invited to address Hazel's guests, he put a muddy shoe on one of her armchairs and gave an impassioned speech emphasizing two themes: that capitalism was the best economic system, and only needed tinkering around the edges, and that the only way to avoid another world war (this emphasized by pounding one fist in the other hand) was to do what we did in 1787: "federate." The looks of horror on the faces of his listeners as he broached these themes were quite wonderful to behold; they asked few questions, and melted quietly into the London fog. I don't think Hazel ever quite understood what had happened.

1951 was an election year in the United Kingdom. Labour had won the general election of 1950, but with a majority of only six seats over the combined opposition. Atlee found it impossible to govern under these conditions, especially since the Tories prolonged sessions of the House of Commons beyond the last underground trains, forcing Labour members to spend the nights on cots in St. Stephens Hall (the Tories, or at least many of them, had apartments in the high-rent Borough of Westminster, within an easy walk of the House). So Atlee called another general election for the fall of 1951, and I had a chance to observe a campaign, British-style, at close quarters. What I chiefly admired was the brevity and the low cost; only five weeks elapsed between the time Atlee called on the King for a writ of election and Election Day itself, and the parties were strictly limited in what they could spend. The Tories won, with a majority of thirty, and installed an elderly Churchill as Prime Minister and Eden, the heir apparent, as Foreign Secretary.

I spent most of my spare time that year in the Strangers Gallery of the House of Commons. Question period was the most fun. One day, while a junior Tory minister was having trouble with a parliamentary inquiry, Churchill entered the chamber. All eyes were on him as he shuffled toward the front bench, and the House subsided into an uncharacteristic silence. At this moment a Labour member jumped to his feet: "Mr. Speaker, why beat on the monkey when the organ grinder is now in our midst?" Alas, Congress offers nothing comparable.

My infatuation with the parliamentary system has probably hindered rather than helped me politically. I lack the skills needed to woo voters en masse, having once been described by a friend as having all the political sex appeal of a snapping turtle. But in a parliamentary system, where advancement depends more on the esteem of one's colleagues than on the adulation of the crowd, my asperity might have been less of a handicap. Cast loose in the colder waters of American politics I was dependent on luck , which did not altogether desert me, but it made for a much more precarious political life.

Coming back from England in June of 1952 to serve as best man at my sister's marriage to my college roommate I concluded that the Army would eventually get me, so I beat them to the punch by enlisting. Though a Quaker since my sophomore year in college, I was not (nor am I today) a thoroughgoing pacifist. One day in 1957 when I was standing next to Cardinal Cushing at a reception in his honor at Phillips Brooks House, he turned to me and asked, "Are you one of my flock?" "No," I replied, "I'm a Quaker." "Ah, then you are a pacifist." "No, I am a non-pacifist Quaker." "Aha – then you are a heresy within a heresy within a heresy." That continues to be a good description of my status.

The Army was an important part of my political education. I regret that privileged young people like myself are no longer subject to the humanizing influence of having to live and work with a cross-section of their peers. I was sent for basic training to Fort Indiantown Gap, Pennsylvania, only two hours from the farm. It was there that I passed the 1952 presidential campaign, voting for Adlai Stevenson by absentee military ballot. The quality of political discourse in Company I, Third Battalion was not high. Democrats promoted the view that since Ike was a general he was bound to screw enlisted men; Republicans countered with the argument that if Stevenson couldn't handle his wife (they were divorced), he couldn't handle the country. So much for an informed electorate.

An amusing post-script to the 1952 campaign occurred in 1957. I was then a student at the Harvard Law School, having decided that an Army career was not for me. During the 1956 campaign I co-chaired the Cambridge Volunteers for Stevenson, along with Miriam Schlesinger, then the wife of Arthur Schlesinger, Jr., one of my former professors. We had the dubious distinction of losing Cambridge for the first time in the 20th century for a Democratic presidential candidate. Sometime after the 1956 election when Governor Stevenson came to Cambridge to see his son, Adlai III, who was a year or two ahead of me in law school, I was invited to a cocktail party in his honor. I managed to corner him, and to say: "Governor, I can't understand how you lost the '52 election: I voted for you seven times!" His eyes bulged with curiosity. I explained that I had solicited absentee ballots for several of my Democratic messmates, one in New York, one in Pennsylvania (in addition to my own) and four in West Virginia, and helped my companions fill them out. The Governor thanked me, and said that if a million other people had done the same he would have won the election.

At the end of Law School I faced a fateful decision: where to practice law. I had overtures from one of the big Philadelphia firms, but I had spent the summer between my second and third years with the firm of Barley, Snyder, Cooper and Mueller in Lancaster, Pennsylvania, twenty-seven miles from the farm. My mother had been diagnosed in 1957 as having cancer of the colon; my father, who was nearly 80 by then, was in no condition to look after her, and my sister and her husband had moved to Colorado. It seemed necessary to be close to the family and the farm, so in the fall of 1958 I moved to Lancaster County – an unlikely venue for an aspiring Democratic politician. I was a Democrat in a highly Republican county; I was a product of Phillips Exeter Academy, Harvard College, Harvard Law School and the London School of Economics (the local state university would have been a much safer credential); and I was a bachelor in a community that professed devotion to what are currently called "family values," not a resumé that would make a campaign manager salivate.

But my principal disqualification, as I discovered slowly and painfully over the next 45 years, was none of these circumstances, but a certain cast of mind. As I look back to 1958 I discern the following premises of my thinking about politics; never articulated, they were nonetheless real:

1. Appeals to reason and compassion will ordinarily prevail over self-interest.

2. All questions of public policy should be decided "on the merits;" "deals" are suspect as being corrupt.

3. Brains and formal education count for more than experience and common sense.

4. People who disagree with you are either knaves or fools

5. Most questions of public policy can be solved through a combination of empirical research and application of correct theory; and therefore,

6. Progress is not only possible, but inevitable.

These preconceptions were not, as it turned out, much help in understanding the world I was about to enter; they amounted to an anti-political theory of politics, a modern version of Plato's philosopher-king, with the king's role being taken by an educated elite. This theory is to be contrasted with the much more realistic understandings that underlay the drafting of the U.S. Constitution as set forth in the Federalist Papers. Madison and Hamilton understood that people inevitably pursue their self-interest; that unless restrained they will do so to the destruction of other points of view; and that the best way to prevent this from happening is to construct a government in which "ambition must be made to counteract ambition." Call this, for lack of a better term, a pragmatic theory of politics.

Where did my preconceptions come from? Certainly not from my father, who was a horse-trader from way back; but then he never discussed politics, or much of anything else, for that matter, with my sister and myself. Perhaps, to some extent, from my mother, who was the product of the brand of idealism associated with Professor Robert Brooks of the Swarthmore political science department. It must have been reinforced, or at least not contradicted, by my various teachers at Exeter and Harvard, although Oscar Handlin, my undergraduate thesis advisor, concealed beneath a very academic demeanor a deep interest in and understanding of practical politics, especially in Boston and Massachusetts.

Being raised in an academic community doubtless contributed to my somewhat otherworldly views. I have the highest respect for scholarship and teaching, but they don't generally breed qualities useful in public life; Woodrow Wilson was elected President in spite of his having been a Princeton professor, not because of it. I was once accosted on the Franklin and Marshall College campus in Lancaster by a colleague who berated me for a vote I had cast in Harrisburg the previous week. I explained the complexity of the issues involved, and then asked, "How would you have voted?" "I would have abstained," was the triumphant reply.

Quakerism may also have played a role. I had become a member of the Society of Friends as a college sophomore, not from any sudden access of piety, but because it seemed to me to be the most humane and the least theologically objectionable of the Protestant churches. American Friends have been deeply ambivalent about

Quaker involvement in public life; the schism between Orthodox and Hicksite Friends in the 1800s was, in part, a dispute about that very question. The Orthodox Friends withdrew entirely from politics, with consequences laid out most graphically in E. Digby Baltzell's "Puritan Boston and Quaker Philadelphia." But even the Hicksite Friends, who were theoretically less hostile to public life, tended to see most issues in moral terms, which made compromise difficult.

Another dimension of Quakerism, which may have contributed to the unreality of my early mind-set, stems from what is perhaps its central tenet, that there is "that of God in every person." This belief has had some admirable consequences, leading Quakers, for example, to decry slavery and to take a central role in prison reform. But it overlooks the fact that the human heart is also a region of darker impulses, many of them, so current research suggests, the residue of our evolutionary history. Madison and his colleagues understood clearly that human nature, unchecked, could lead to disastrous results. He says, in Federalist No. 51: "It may be a reflection on human nature, that such devices [checks and balances] should be necessary to control the abuses of government. But what is government itself, but the greatest of all reflections on human nature."

One way of describing this cast of mind is to call me at 28 an "idealist," i.e., someone who has a mental picture of the world and thinks he can make the real world conform to his picture. I'm not sure that I was ever quite so naive as that, but I certainly harbored a number of illusions which, if I had clung to them over the next forty years, would have guaranteed my political ineffectiveness. The story of my political education is, then, largely the story of the shedding of those illusions and the acquisition, much too late in life, of a more useful set of premises.

Chapter 2 - Getting My Feet Wet

As a place to live and work Lancaster County has the virtues and defects of its predominantly German population. Its inhabitants are tidy, thrifty and hard-working, resulting in a prosperous and generally law-abiding society. On the downside they are apt to be intolerant of people who look, speak, or think differently; growing Hispanic and African American communities, concentrated in the City of Lancaster, are not well integrated into the larger society. And there is a certain lack of creativity, an unwillingness to depart from customary ways of thinking and acting, that leads many of our best and brightest young people to seek fame and fortune elsewhere.

I began practicing law in Lancaster in September of 1958 in the very Republican firm of Barley, Snyder, Cooper, and Mueller, where I had clerked the summer before. The founder of the firm, Paul Mueller, Sr. had died during my third year at law school; Ralph Barley, a wise man and a scrupulously good lawyer, took over as senior partner. Dick Snyder, former newspaperman, then Republican county chairman and later a state senator was a key figure -- bright, partisan, acerbic. Charles Cooper and Paul Mueller, Jr. were the other partners. Paul, a Princeton graduate, had been a year behind me at Exeter and was my entry to the firm. Jack Barber and I were the two associates. Although I had been called 'Jack' from birth, Jack Barber seemed to have acquired the rights to that name so I readily acquiesced in being called "John."

I rented an apartment on the third floor of a building three blocks from the Franklin and Marshall College campus and six blocks from the law office. My apartment was in the Fourth Precinct of the Ninth Ward. Under party rules prevailing at the time each precinct was entitled to a committeeman and a committeewoman elected by the registered Democrats in the precinct for a two-year term. Our precinct had a committeewoman -- the redoubtable Marguerite Herrold -- but no committeeman. So I volunteered, and was duly appointed to fill the vacancy. That led eventually to my being elected leader of the Ninth Ward and thus a member of the County Executive Committee.

It is perhaps appropriate, since the rest of this book is about my involvement with the Democratic Party, to say something about my own view of American political parties.

Although I have voted for only two Republicans in 50 years, I am not quite a yellow dog Democrat. I simply concluded a long time ago that our system works best if most citizens identify strongly with one of the two major parties and then work within that party to shape it in accordance with their views of public policy. Since I also concluded that I was basically a liberal, it was natural for me to make my home within the Democratic Party. But as odd as it may seem, I have more in common with my Republican neighbors who serve their party in a variety of ways than with the Ralph Naders of this world who have nothing but contempt for the two major parties. Politics without parties strikes me, to borrow a phrase from Robert Frost, as tennis without a net.

Otherwise intelligent people tell me that they will contribute money to individual candidates but not to a political party. That seems short-sighted. Economists talk about what they call "The Tragedy of the Commons." If you are a peasant in 15th century England who is hauling manure out of his barn in the Spring, you have two choices: you can put the manure on your own strips of land, held on feudal tenure from the Lord of the Manor, or you can put it on the commons where you and the other peasants pasture your cows and sheep, sharing a joint responsibility for the pasturage and the fences. The easy choice is to put the manure on your own land, where the benefits will accrue within the year to you and to you alone. But if you and your neighbors all make the same decision, the commons will suffer: its pasturage will decline, its fences will fall down, the wolves will devour the lambs and the calves, and the village will go into decline. And all this because of a decision that while rational in terms of your short-term interests is disastrous for the community in the long run.

Political parties are the commons of the American political system. A rational candidate with money to invest will put it into his own campaign, rather than the party. But the cumulative effect of this decision being made over and over again is to weaken if not destroy the party – and with it the capacity to register voters, staff the polling places, distribute literature, recruit candidates, and perform all the other services that American parties, without much fanfare, have been rendering for the better part of two centuries.

Mike Sturla, the Democrat who now represents my old House district, the 96th, typifies the more far-sighted view of the relationship between an elected official and his party. His district continues to be one of the more marginal House seats; in some years the local Republican party has spent upwards of $150,000 in an unsuccessful effort to unseat him. Sturla's reelection hinges at least in part on Republican ticket-splitters in the more affluent precincts on the edge of the city. Under these conditions the smart thing would be for Sturla to keep his distance from the Democratic Party. But, to the contrary, he does everything in his power to shore up the party, not just in the 96th but in the suburban and rural parts of the county as well. I can't begin to count the number of times he has called me to report having met someone from New Holland or Ephrata or Lititz who might be interested in getting involved in local Democratic politics. Mike thus demonstrates his understanding of the fact that the wise farmer spreads the manure on the commons (i.e., the political party) as well as his own strips of land.

As De Tocqueville pointed out 170 years ago, the underlying strength of America derives less from its governmental structures than from the dense network of voluntary associations, political parties among them, which provide training in self-government. Recent commentators, such as Robert Putnam ("Bowling Alone") and Robert Bellah et al. ("Habits of the Heart") claim to have discerned a weakening of these associations in the past twenty years. That conclusion would certainly be justified in the case of political parties as we witness lower turnouts for elections, difficulty in recruiting committee people, and a growing number of uncontested seats both in Congress and in our state legislatures.

Ascertaining the reasons for this decline in civic participation is less easy. Putnam is inclined to point to TV – what he calls the "privatization of leisure" – as a major culprit. Others indict the one-parent family and the two-working-parent family. Whether the increasing professionalization of political campaigns is cause or effect, or both, is not clear; is television advertising needed because people can't be recruited to go door-to-door, or do the ads diminish the incentive to canvass? Even the well-intentioned Motor Voter Act, by appearing to relieve the parties of responsibility for voter registration, may be partly to blame. And I hope I'm not being partisan in saying that derogation of government by conservatives, even those holding public office, hasn't helped.

Some responsibility for this state of affairs surely rests with the press, print as well as TV, which on the whole does a poor job of covering politics and government, especially at the state level. Choosing to entertain rather than to educate, the press emphasizes the simple over the complex, the ephemeral over the durable, the emotional over the cerebral and the process ("who's ahead") over the result ("what does it mean?"). Given the inherent complexity of many of the issues now confronting us, it is no wonder that the citizenry often appears befuddled.

The essence of politics is compromise, something not well understood either by the media or the general public (or by my earlier self), which continue to speak disparagingly of "wheeling and dealing;" the assumption seems to be that each issue should be decided "on the merits," without respect to any other issue which is part of the current scene. An editorial from the Philadelphia Inquirer provides an illuminating example of this cast of mind. In 1980, the Pennsylvania Senate Democrats faced a difficult problem: because they were in a minority, they stood to lose out in the decennial reapportionment which was about to take place. Much hinged on the fifth member of the reapportionment commission, who would be the swing vote. At the same time the Senate Republican majority was trying to line up the two-thirds vote needed to confirm Bruce Kauffman, a distinguished Philadelphia lawyer, to a permanent position on the State Supreme Court. The Senate Democrats said, in effect, "we won't contribute any votes for Kauffman until we are assured of a fifth member on the reapportionment commission whom we can trust."

This stance evoked a stern editorial rebuke from the Inquirer, which criticized the linking of two logically unrelated issues. But what the editorial is really denouncing is the political process itself, the attempt to derive whatever advantages you can from the situation you find yourself in. The minority Democrats had few bargaining chips in this situation; blocking Kauffman's confirmation was one of them. To denounce this coupling of "logically unrelated issues" is simply fatuous and shows that the Inquirer editorial board was in about the same primitive frame of mind I was in at the age of 28.

As politics is the art of compromise, a successful politician needs to cultivate as many ties as she can, in order to enlarge the number of compromises that are possible. "Networking" was invented by politicians long before sociologists gave a name to the activity. Abner Mikva, a Congressman who was later a judge of the District of Columbia Court of Appeals, tells a story about volunteering to work in one of Mayor Daley's Chicago campaigns. The ward heeler behind the desk had one question: "Who sent you?" Mikva: "nobody." Politician: "we don't want nobody that nobody sent." When I recounted this story to my Franklin and Marshall students, asking what was Mikva's mistake, the usual reply was, "he should have had a letter of recommendation." This somewhat misses the point; a letter of recommendation from one of his college professors would not likely have advanced his cause. What he needed was a recommendation from someone who was either owed a favor by the Daley machine or whom the machine wanted to put under some future obligation; someone who walks in off the street meets neither of these tests.

At any rate, by 1958 I had identified myself as a Democrat who would be happiest working within the party. Sometime that winter I paid a call on the city's most illustrious Democrat, Mayor Thomas J. Monaghan, an ebullient Irishman from Mahanoy City in the anthracite coal region, then serving the first of three terms as mayor. Midway through our conversation the telephone rang; the mayor apologized for taking the call, and his end of the ensuing conversation went something like this:

M - What? A pothole?

M - How big?

M - What block of Lafayette St.? I'll be right there!

He hung up, told me to wait, and rushed out. He was back in 30 minutes beaming with satisfaction. I asked if the mayor supervised the filling of every pothole in the city. His reply: "No, but there are 13 votes in that family!"

The next year the Mayor gave me the unenviable task of running the re-election campaign of Herb Wagaman, the Minority County Commissioner. In Pennsylvania the three county commissioners who combine legislative and executive functions to run the county are elected under a system that while ostensibly guaranteeing minority representation actually gives the majority party a strong voice in the selection of the minority commissioner. Each party nominates two candidates, and in November voters cast two votes, the top three candidates being elected. On the surface this appears to guarantee minority representation, but the reality is far different. In Lancaster County the two Democrats who emerge victorious from the primary quickly perceive that only one of them can win, so they campaign quietly against each other, guaranteeing that both won't win. To make matters worse the Republican Party, knowing that if everyone votes a straight party ticket they will carry the county by at least 2-1, and calculating which of the two Democrats will be more tractable, throws a few votes to that person in selected precincts. The result is often a Board of Commissioners that contains no one who can speak forcefully for the county's 70,000 registered Democrats.

Wagaman suited the Republicans just fine. He was a lanky ex-semi pro basketball player from the Lititz area who spoke with a pronounced Pennsylvania Dutch accent. My job was to see to it that he reached whatever events he was scheduled to take part in each weekend. I failed as often as I succeeded, but he was re-elected anyway, doubtless with Republican assistance.

Another incident in Mayor Monaghan's office yields some insight into his operating methods. I listened one day in some astonishment as he offered the job of chairman of one of the city authorities to a businessman with a dubious reputation. The offer was refused. When he slapped the phone down with a self-satisfied grin I blurted out, "I can't believe what I just heard." "Oh, I knew he would turn it down," came the reply; "but he will tell everybody at the Elks that I offered him the job." Franklin D. Roosevelt is supposed to have offered the post of Ambassador to Poland to six or seven people before giving it to the man who was his first choice all along. This sort of maneuvering takes more self-confidence than I have ever felt.

In the 1960s much of our time at city committee meetings was devoted to patronage, now pretty much wiped out except at the highest levels by a combination of civil service and municipal unions. Inevitably some committeeman would say, in Mayor Monaghan's presence, "How come Schwartz is still working in the Water Department when his wife is a Republican Committeewoman?" That would unleash a torrent of recriminations, since some committee members had been attracted to politics in the first instance by the lure of public employment.

I had been disabused about the virtues of civil service at an early age. Mary Temple Newman, a Swarthmore College graduate who once worked for my father, invited me to Sunday dinner in Cambridge when I was a law student. Mary had been elected to the Massachusetts House of Representatives from Cambridge, and later served in Governor Francis Sargent's cabinet. I was pontificating about the evils of patronage when Mary broke in: "Jack, do you know what is the only department of state government that answers their phones after 5 p.m.?" I confessed I had no idea. "Motor Vehicles. And do you know why? Because they are staffed with political employees; the civil servants all go home on the dot of 5 p..m." Well, maybe; but I have known a good many civil servants who put in far more time than they were paid to do.

In the end I prefer civil service for a different reason than the ones usually advanced: most patronage under modern conditions is more trouble than it is worth. I remember arguing with Governor Milton Shapp about a bill that I would have supported but he opposed, which would have transferred the operations of the state college system out of the Department of Education to an independent agency. I liked the fact that it would have given the colleges more autonomy; he was bemoaning the prospective loss of his power to appoint the presidents of the 14 colleges. I told him, by way of reply, that each appointment won him one dubiously loyal friend and ten bitter enemies. He was unpersuaded. The bill later passed in the Thornburg Administration and has fulfilled neither my hopes nor Shapp's fears.

One feature of the gradual disappearance of patronage from the political scene is to be regretted: it was jobs that tied many working-class American families to one of the two great political parties. They were more interested in jobs than in policies. The elimination of patronage is probably one of the reasons for the slow decline in participation in electoral politics; it has turned off many rank and file voters and enlarged the role of what our British friends call the "chattering classes," who support civil service reform because in their not wholly disinterested view it rewards merit in the only form in which they recognize it, i.e., formal education.

Beginning in December 1959, John Hartman and Bob Pfannebecker, two young Democratic attorneys in Lancaster County, undertook to conduct workshops for Democratic committee people using materials and techniques perfected by the Kennedys. The materials included a film on door-to-door canvassing (unfortunately, from our viewpoint, filmed in a Chicago apartment house) sponsored by the Independent Voters of Illinois. John became well enough known through these workshops to become a plausible candidate for county chairman, a position to which he was duly elected in June of 1960.

John and I spent most of our weekends that summer driving around Lancaster County, recruiting committee people. 1960 was a fascinating year in which to be involved in Democratic politics in Lancaster County. Our delegate to the Democratic Convention in Los Angeles was George Winterling, the Mayor's chief fund-raiser and a thoroughgoing iconoclast. One hot summer evening as we sat in the kitchen of the Hartmans' home on Burrowes Avenue – John, his wife Joyce, Bob Pfannebecker, and myself – Winterling called from the convention for advice. I was still for Stevenson, for all the wrong reasons, but the others were intrigued by Kennedy. In the end we told George to use his best judgment, this being back in the days when convention delegates were permitted to think for themselves.

The 1960 campaign in Lancaster County was marred by virulent anti-Catholic sentiment, aimed in part at activating the historically anti-papist prejudices of the Anabaptist churches. One Mennonite lawyer, with offices in the same building as Democratic Headquarters, appeared to be spending most of his time mailing out tracts warning against the coming take-over by the Pope. The Amish, historically opposed to involvement in public life, registered to vote in substantial numbers. Kennedy came to Lancaster on tour in September and addressed a wildly enthusiastic crowd of 7,500 in Penn Square, but that was dwarfed by the 30,000 who turned out to greet Nixon in October.

We were apprehensive - and with good reason. Nixon carried Lancaster County by 45,157 votes. But his margin here and elsewhere in central Pennsylvania was eclipsed by huge Democratic pluralities in Philadelphia, Pittsburgh and the coal regions. JFK carried Pennsylvania by 116,326 votes and took the presidency in a very close election.

The 1960 election may have spelled my doom, however, with Barley, Snyder, Cooper and Mueller. I had been scrupulous in telling Ralph Barley that I was not only a Democrat but likely to be an active one, though I promised not to politick on office time -- a promise I kept. But my activities must have been increasingly irritating to some of the firm's corporate clients, especially the Armstrong Cork Company, then the dominant force in the county, both economically and politically.

The Republican Party in Lancaster County works hard to squelch any possible opposition. One example from my own experience will suggest the lengths to which it will go. Walking across the Franklin and Marshall College campus one day in the mid-sixties I met Keith Spalding, then President of the College, and the person who chiefly guided Franklin and Marshall College to its present eminence among small liberal arts colleges. Beginning in 1961, I had taught there occasionally as an untenured adjunct in the Government Department, mostly sections of the basic course on American Government, filling in for faculty who were ill or on sabbatical.

Keith said, "Pitt, there's something I have wanted to tell you for a long time but I couldn't make up my mind whether telling you would be a service or a disservice. I had a call last year from Bill Schnader (senior partner in the Philadelphia law firm of Schnader, Segal, Harrison, and Lewis; unsuccessful Republican candidate for governor in 1934; and chairman of the Franklin and Marshall College Board of Trustees), asking if I would fire you. I told Schnader that I didn't interfere with academic appointments of that sort, and I have heard nothing since."

I was flabbergasted. Apparently someone in the local Republican leadership had called Schnader asking him to put pressure on the college to get rid of me. I hadn't realized I was that dangerous. I prefer to think that the current leadership of the Republican Party would not go so far, but they have shown a disturbing tendency to cut corners, as for example, in violating laws relating to voter registration.

The overt hostility of Armstrong and other major employers seriously affected our ability to recruit party workers and candidates. For example, Hartman and I had decided to recruit as a candidate for the city school board a mid-level executive at Armstrong, who was himself a graduate of J.P. McCaskey, the city high school, and who had a son then enrolled in the school. When approached, his reply was: "Boys, I'd like to do it, but you know where I work." And this from a corporation whose top executives were constantly making speeches about freedom and the American way of life. Armstrong executives would doubtless deny that they had any policy to discourage employees from being active Democrats ("there's nothing in writing"), but the widespread belief to the contrary belies their protestations.

Another incident will illustrate the weak Lancaster County attachment to civil liberties. I had agreed to be a preceptor for a young man who had applied for admission to the bar. One day I was stopped on Duke Street by Alex Stein, a fellow attorney and chairman of the committee which evaluated candidates. Alex reported that his committee "had a problem" with my young protégé because he had taken part in demonstrations against the Vietnam War. I said to Alex, "If your committee rejects him for that reason, I will take the case to the Supreme Court of the United States; I will win – and it will cost the Bar Association $50,000." Not long afterwards the young man was approved by the committee.

Ralph Barley took me to dinner at the Hamilton Club in the summer of 1961 and told me that the time had come for me to make a choice between law and politics. He spoke well of my work as a lawyer, but disparagingly of my activities in the political arena. I pointed out that his partner Dick Snyder was the Republican County chairman and that nobody had asked him to make the same choice: a good debating point, but not very persuasive under the circumstances.

I took only a few days to make up my mind, and resigned from the firm. John Hartman and I agreed to share office space and a secretary beginning after Labor Day. It was a terrible gamble for both of us: John had a wife and seven daughters to support, and I, though single, had no network of family and friends in the county who could be counted upon to bring their legal problems to me. We both survived- just barely. But I had learned an important lesson: in the immortal words of Mr. Dooley, "Politics ain't beanbag."

Chapter 3 - In the Trenches

The key figure on the local political scene, at least before the era dominated by television, was the precinct committeeperson. In Pennsylvania there are about 10,000 precincts or voting districts; each is run by two committee people, now elected by the Democrats for four-year terms and by the Republicans for two-year terms. A precinct generally has between 500 and 2000 voters. In a large city it may be no more than three or four blocks square; in a sparsely settled rural area it may be fifty square miles. Whatever the size, it is the basic unit of the political system.

By now, I have been a precinct committeeman for 24 of my 50 adult years: for twelve years in the densely populated Ninth Ward, Fourth Precinct of Lancaster City; for eight years in the sparsely settled rural precinct of West Nottingham Township in Chester County; and more recently in the suburban precinct of Rohrerstown, East Hempfield Township, Lancaster County. Of all the purely political (as opposed to public) positions I have held, being a committeeman is probably the one that has given me the most satisfaction. There are two explanations, I think: the fact that the results of your labors are palpable, and the stimulation afforded by daily encounters with the human race in its infinite variety.

As far as results are concerned, nothing beats the Nancy Cox saga. In 1989 I helped persuade Nancy, a neighbor and long-time friend, to run for supervisor in West Nottingham Township. Around 4 p.m. on Election Day, I stopped by the polling place, picking up the names of the Democrats who had already voted. Back at the farm house, I began calling the others. The message was simple: "Get your butt up to the Grange before 8 o'clock – Nancy needs your help." As it turned out, Nancy won, 197-191: not exactly a landslide, but a victory nonetheless. Nancy went on to serve another term as supervisor, and then lost to an incumbent Republican in an ugly legislative race in 2002 and again in 2004. It doesn't take many outcomes like that one to compensate for the time and energy expended in local politics.

My enjoyment of the committeeman's role has made it hard for me to understand why it is increasingly difficult to recruit people for these jobs. But the facts are inescapable. In Philadelphia the Republican Party is unrepresented in about half the city divisions (which is what they call a precinct); here in Lancaster County the Democratic Party is seldom able to fill more than 300 out of 450 positions, and many of the 300 are inactive. Why the problem? The widespread, and apparently increasing public contempt for politics and politicians plays a role. So does the family in which both parents work, and the one-parent family; neither leaves much of a margin for the assumption of civic responsibility. But the chief culprit, in my judgment, is the triumph of the private over the public sphere, a triumph encouraged by President Reagan and the two Bushes. The results are brilliantly recorded in Robert Putnam's book, "Bowling Alone," charting the decline in political and many other forms of civic activity.

The best way to understand the life of a committee person is to see it in cyclical terms. In January one faces the need to recruit candidates for local office, including township supervisors and borough council members, mayors, auditors, constables, tax collectors, district justices and school board candidates. Reformers have long advocated the "short ballot" and would chastise Pennsylvania for including auditors (and coroners!) among the elective offices. If efficiency is the only test, they are probably right; an appointed CPA is likely to perform the audit more expeditiously (and more expensively) than a three-person board with no expertise. On the other hand, the position of auditor affords a bird's-eye view of township government to three people at a modest expenditure of time and energy; many elected auditors have gone on to be supervisors, borough council members and even legislators. So there are trade-offs.

Finding suitable school board candidates has become especially tricky, even though the Pennsylvania legislature has reduced the term of office from six years to four; the work is so time-consuming, and the tax and labor relations issues so acute, it's a wonder any sensible people can be found to shoulder the burdens. I have the impression, unsupported by any scientific evidence, that the quality of school board members has been declining steadily in recent years, as pillar-of-the-community types give way to one-issue zealots, people concerned only with holding the line on taxes or opposing sex education or fielding a winning football team.

February in Pennsylvania brings ice, snow and nominating conventions: gatherings of committee people to endorse candidates for regional and county offices. In the majority party, these may be quite spirited affairs, with complex party rules governing the number of votes necessary to secure the coveted party 'endorsement;' in the minority party, it is more often a question of who will be the sacrificial lamb. Thus in 1999 I volunteered to run for County Treasurer, spending only $298 (on a newspaper ad with my cat) in losing by 23,000 votes. But at least the Democratic position on the ballot didn't say, as it so often does in Lancaster County, "No candidate."

In March the snow and ice thaw and so does the political scene. Nominating petitions must be circulated, often in foul weather, requiring anywhere from five signatures (some local offices) to one thousand (Congress). Pennsylvania is a "closed primary" state, i.e., only registered Republicans may vote in the Republican primary and only registered Democrats may vote in the Democratic primary, but an exception is made for school board candidates and district justices who may cross file. Some voter registration takes place, although the major drives are in late summer and early Fall. Committee people make sure that all positions on the precinct Election Boards, the group that supervises the conduct of the election, are filled, something we are more alert to after the debacle of 2000 in Florida. And the more energetic committee persons recruit watchers for inside the polling place, leafletters for outside and one or more persons to telephone those who haven't shown up by late afternoon.

Primary Day in Pennsylvania is in May, except in presidential years, when it is in April. In West Nottingham elections were a very social event, one of the few occasions when the inhabitants of a rural community encountered any substantial number of their fellow citizens. It was all very cordial. We voted in a ramshackle frame building belonging to the local chapter of the Grange. The ladies of the Grange served a hearty lunch -- chicken, mashed potatoes, creamed mushrooms, peas and several homemade pies - at $5 per head. The Board, watchers, leafletters and local party officials partook, joined occasionally by candidates and some of our more eminent office holders. On several occasions we had a visit from Stanley, a donkey who was the mascot of the local Democratic Party and who placidly endured all sorts of political taunts.

The aim of the primary, of course, is to ensure that the endorsed candidates win. This requires that you accost as many of your own voters as possible on their way into the Grange, with a palm card ("Cox for Supervisor - #19B on your Democratic ballot") or other reminder. Some voters object to running a gauntlet of candidates and party workers on their way into the polling place. Their objections have been endorsed by state legislatures and by the Supreme Court of the United States. The Court, in what I think was an unwise decision, upheld a Tennessee statute prohibiting campaigning within one hundred feet of a polling place (in Pennsylvania you need only put 10 feet between yourself and the entrance to the polls). I blame the plaintiffs lawyers as much as I blame the Court, however, because they obviously did a poor job of showing the practical impact of such a limitation. In West Nottingham, a 100-foot rule would relegate workers to the paved road approaching the Grange; no one could electioneer in the grass parking lot adjacent to the Grange where everyone parks. This is a serious drawback, especially for local candidates lacking the resources to campaign by mail. Being accosted on your way to vote is a small price to pay for a vigorous democracy; the Court, so sensitive to free speech considerations in other contexts, is surprisingly insensitive here.

Sometimes I think that Americans, just as they believe in economic competition as long as it does not apply to them, so they believe in democracy as long as the inconvenience is visited on someone else. Recently the Residents' Council at the retirement community where my wife and I live voted 9-7 to bar any appearance on our campus by candidates or public officials, in the interest of preserving harmony in our community. I suspect that if it had been up to my fellow residents the American Revolution would never have taken place; it would have been too upsetting to their Tory neighbors.

After the primary comes a welcome lull -- perhaps a workshop for new committee people or a fund-raiser and, once every four years, a convention to elect a county chairman and other officers -- but otherwise the doldrums. Summer is the time to get started on voter registration – at one time the most important responsibility of a committee person.

A good deal of nonsense has been written in recent years on the subject of voter registration. A book by two left-wing academics, Richard Cloward and Frances Fox Piven, describes a capitalist plot to put difficulties in the way of poor and uneducated people who want to register and vote. The truth is less dramatic, but in some ways more discouraging and, ultimately, more supportive of their Marxist analysis. Large numbers of people don't register, or if they are registered, don't vote, because they don't give a damn; they are convinced that their votes are meaningless. I could not begin to count the number of times I have sat at someone's kitchen table, registration form open, pen in hand, only to be told, "We don't believe in that shit," or "They're all crooks" or "It don't make no difference what I do." The latter, I think, comes closest to the truth: a substantial number of Pennsylvanians think that the political process has gotten far beyond their ability to influence. I wish I were more certain that they are wrong.

As Americans, I don't think we've begun to come to grips with the fact that the electorate has expanded beyond anything Madison and his colleagues might have imagined. The debates in the Convention were between those who thought democracy possible only in small communities like Athens, where the population eligible to vote has been estimated at around five thousand, and those who thought it could work even better in a nation the size of the new United States of America in 1787. But we now face a potential electorate of over 200 million with 115 million votes having been cast in the presidential election of 2004.

I submit that this is a change in degree which amounts, in fact, to a change in kind, undermining many of the assumptions on which the Madisonian "solution" is based. It is no longer possible to think of a voting public listening to what candidates say on the hustings, reading what is written about them in the local press, and casting their votes accordingly. The most effective way to reach an electorate of this size is through television; and the 2004 presidential campaign is showing us how degraded a campaign conducted chiefly by means of paid TV ads can be. The techniques for obscuring the truth are multiplying faster than the means of uncovering it. Add to this brew the increasing complexity of issues involved and I find it hard to argue (though I do so vigorously) with the citizen who says, "I abstain."

In 1993 Congress, attempting to increase voter turnout, passed what has come to be known as the 'Motor Voter Act.' Its central feature requires states to allow people to register to vote as part of the process of getting a motor vehicle license or signing up for welfare or unemployment benefits. So far it seems to have resulted in substantial (but not massive) increases in voter registration, with no clear advantage to either party nationwide. But the higher number of registered voters has not translated into higher voter turnout. And one negative effect of the Act, at least for those of us who have to make the system work, stems from a provision prohibiting states from purging voters who don't vote regularly except by a complex and costly process once every eight years. As a result, our voter lists are cluttered with an increasing number of people who in fact no longer live where they are registered but who cannot be taken off the list, and parties and candidates waste precious hours trying to contact, by telephone, or precious dollars trying to reach, by mail, people who simply aren't there.

There are various ways of locating unregistered voters -- phone calls to registered voters; tables at malls; paying attention to new construction and 'For Sale' signs -- but in the end there is only one really good way, and that is going door-to-door. In canvassing you not only uncover partisans who can be registered, but a wealth of other information as well: who has moved, who needs an absentee ballot or a ride to the polls, what a voter thinks about a certain candidate or issue, and what Republicans are closet Democrats and vice versa.

I have the impression that canvassing is nearly an extinct art. Politicians boast about how many doorbells they have rung, but those boasts are more in the nature of a bow to the folklore than a description of present activity. What has supplanted canvassing is electronic politics: computers, polls, phone banks, direct mail and radio and television spots. With computers it is possible to target mail or phone calls to particular audiences: pro-choice Republican women under fifty, for example, or Democrats who have voted in at least four of the last ten elections. The problem with this approach is that it simply reinforces current voting patterns. Sarah Gunzenhauser doesn't vote very often; the computer therefore treats her as someone who is not worth a letter or a phone call; since she doesn't receive a letter or phone call, she is barely aware that an election is taking place, and doesn't vote, all but ensuring that she will be ignored again next time around.

There are some signs, in 2004, that parties and candidates are re-thinking how they allocate scarce campaign resources, spending less on television advertisements and more on voter registration and getting out the vote; it remains to be seen whether this is genuine change. Governor Dean's successful use of the internet to energize his supporters as well as raise money adds a new dimension to modern campaigning. But I am an agnostic about the end results.

Nor is this vicious cycle neutral in terms of its effects on the two major political parties. All the academic evidence points to the fact that education and income are directly related to the frequency of voting. Since Democratic voters tend to be less prosperous and less well educated than Republican voters, a higher proportion of Democratic registrants don't vote, or show up at the polls only for presidential elections. But these are the very ones who are likely to be ignored by the modern scientific campaign, reinforcing, or at least not counteracting, their tendency to stay home.

Another barrier to effective canvassing is the increasing number of voters who are physically inaccessible by virtue of the fact that they live in apartment houses, retirement communities, nursing homes or the latest abomination, "gated" communities. Many of these have policies forbidding door to door solicitation, which presumably includes political canvassing; whether the courts will uphold these policies in the face of challenges based on freedom of speech or association is not clear. One counter stratagem is to recruit a staunch Democrat inside the apartment complex who can go door-to-door without arousing suspicion.

Canvassing helps the candidate or volunteer find out where the voter's loyalties really lie. Once, ringing doorbells on Manor Street in Lancaster City's 8th Ward, I encountered an elderly woman, shabbily dressed. After confirming that she was a registered Republican, I pointed out that she did not have to vote Republican in the general election (I harbor a suspicion that Republicans in Lancaster County are taught from an early age that the voting machine will malfunction or Aunt Susie will haunt them for the rest of their lives if, as registered Republicans, they vote for even one Democratic candidate). Putting her finger to her lips, she pulled me inside and closed the door. "Young man," she cackled, "I've never voted for a Republican in my life." Then why was she registered Republican? "When women got the right to vote they took all of us girls who worked at the Stehli Silk Mill and drove us down to the Court House and registered us Republican." Those were the good old days -- for the Republican Party. The coercion is more subtle these days.

On another occasion, two nuns confessed that, though registered Republican, they generally voted Democratic. I made a note on my canvassing pad. On a rainy election morning, I called to ask if they needed a ride. "Oh, no, thank you, Mr. Santaniello is coming for us at 11." Bernie Santaniello was the Republican committeeman in that precinct; for many years he had been hauling these two citizens to the polls to cast their straight Democratic ballots. (At least I *think* that's what they were doing -- perhaps the joke was on me!)

Door-to-door canvassing yields some other interesting results. I have been propositioned on more than one occasion. An elderly woman declined to register on the grounds that she had promised

43

her husband on his death bed that she would never register or vote. And an elderly man waggled two fingers at me and said (in 1966): "You tell Franklin Roosevelt that I have voted for him for the last time." I didn't have the heart to tell him that FDR had been in his grave for 21 years.

August brings with it the responsibility for organizing the fall fund-raising event, usually a dinner at some local hostelry; the quality of the chicken is generally better than portrayed in the folklore. In Chester County we were harangued by such notables as Ed Rendell, then District Attorney, later Mayor of Philadelphia and Governor of Pennsylvania; Senator Paul Sarbanes of Maryland, a close personal friend; and Harris Wofford, then Pennsylvania's Secretary of Labor and Industry and later (all too briefly) a U.S. Senator.

We usually hope to clear about $2000 from the dinner, 60% of it from ads from sympathetic merchants in a program book and 40% from the sale of tickets. The proceeds are used chiefly to finance the mailing of sample ballots and other campaign material to all registered Democrats before both the primary and general election. Local candidates who want to mail to Republican voters may use the county party's bulk mailing permit but have to raise the money on their own, although beginning in 2001 the Lancaster County Democratic Committee made modest subventions to several local campaigns. One of the pleasant features of local politics is that money is not the sole determinant of success; good candidates and hard work count for at least as much.

September is the occasion for last minute voter registration efforts, the deadline in Pennsylvania being 30 days before the election, and planning for whatever mailing, telephoning, or other campaign activities are required for the general election. October is more or less a repeat of the pre-primary, with even more emphasis on "getting out the vote." In the Rohrerstown precinct where I now live our principal strategy has been to assign each of our telephone volunteers a list of 25-30 registered Democrats to telephone the weekend before the election. It works; in the local election of 2001, the Democratic turnout was 37%, compared to a Republican turnout of 32%. But many voters elude us. Nothing is more distressing than calling a voter at 5 p.m. on election day, only to be offered one of a wide menu of excuses: "I don't feel well;" "We can't find a babysitter"; "My husband (wife) hasn't returned from work, and we always go together;" "The baby is sick;" etc.

Election Day in November comes all too soon; if you are pamphleteering outside the polling place you need to dress more warmly than in May. In Pennsylvania the polls are open from 7 a.m. to 8 p.m. We try to schedule people outside the polls in two-hour shifts so the burdens are shared. In both Rohrerstown and West Nottingham the turnout varied from 300 (primary, off-year) to 700 (general, presidential year) so that for much of the day you are making small talk with the other candidates and workers. Voters stop by my chair as they arrive or leave, sharing observations about the weather, crops, children's progress in school and the low state of American government and politics. The Grange where we voted in

West Nottingham was just across the road from a tidy farm kept by an Amish clan named Stoltzfus, non-voters all; the curving contours of their well-tended fields of tobacco, corn, barley and alfalfa served as a useful reminder that there is more to life than winning or losing elections.

Whatever the outcome, we generally staged a 'victory party' in late November or early December. Even if it has not been a complete victory for our candidates, it has been a victory for the democratic process. As such, it deserves -- and gets -- a cheery celebration, where we thank those who have fought the good fight and begin to think about candidates for the following year. A committeeperson's work is never done.

Chapter 4 - On the Hustings

From my point of view the 1960s might be called "the decade of running strenuously," since I was the Democratic candidate for the 96th Pennsylvania House seat in the City of Lancaster in every election between 1962 and 1970, winning twice and losing three times. My opponent in the first four races was Eugene Rutherford, who owned an electrical appliance store and had been active in the Elks and other civic organizations. In 1970, it was Harold Horn, an insurance broker.

In 1962, no longer afraid of embarrassing my old law firm, I volunteered to be what everyone assumed (correctly, as it turned out) was the sacrificial lamb in a district that last elected a Democrat in 1940. I raised about $2000, campaigned with modest vigor, and lost by 2,127 votes. A victory party at 8th Ward Headquarters turned into a wake. I made a short talk, thanking everyone for their help and promising to do better next time. At that point Joe Ulrich, Jr., the young son of one of our stalwart committeemen, burst into tears: "How can Mr. Pittenger be so cheerful when he lost?" It's not easy explaining that to a 10-year old, but it's worth the effort; graciousness in winning and cheerfulness in losing are among the hallmarks of a healthy democracy.

Two years later there didn't seem to be any reason not to run again. I had run a creditable race in '62; I was bored with my law practice, which was barely keeping me alive; and nobody else seemed in the least bit interested. But the outcome was dramatically different. This time the Democratic ticket was headed by Lyndon Johnson, whose coattails were long; he swept me into office on a vote of 13,682 to 9,497, the largest plurality for a Democratic House candidate in the 20th century. Election night was delirious; we organized an impromptu victory parade, with me riding in the front passenger seat of a convertible. I've always regretted that I was never able to thank Barry Goldwater for helping launch my political career.

The euphoria lasted only two years. Perhaps I was overconfident in 1966; it was a year in which Ray Shafer, who had been Bill Scranton's Lieutenant Governor, carried the state for the Republican ticket by 241,630 votes. At any rate, I lost to Gene Rutherford, whom I had defeated in 1964, by 496 votes, and was plunged into despair.

I thought seriously about returning to the academic world, earning a Ph.D. and teaching full time. But conversations with people at the University of Pennsylvania suggested that they were not going to give me the benefit of the doubt, but would make me jump through the same hoops that they had established for people fresh out of college. A course in legislation was required. Would having been a member of the legislature satisfy the requirement? No. A course in constitutional law was mandatory. Did it help that I was co-author, with Henry Bragdon, of a small book, The Pursuit of Justice, designed for high school civics courses? No. And so on.

My colleagues in the Government Department at Franklin and Marshall College came to my rescue. Sid Wise, Dick Schier, and John Vanderzell had all been advisers to Mayor Monaghan. Sid had worked in the Washington office of Senator Joseph S. Clark (Democrat, Pennsylvania) and had run an outstanding political internship program. Dick had served in the administration of Governor David Lawrence (1959-63) and had twice chaired the Democratic state platform committee. John chaired the City Planning Commission for several years. Their entreaties to Herb Fineman, the very able Philadelphia lawyer who would become minority leader in the next session, paid off; I was offered, and accepted with alacrity, the position of Director of Research for the House Democratic Caucus.

I will postpone to a later chapter a brief discussion of that role. I spent much of my free time during the 1967-68 session getting ready to run once more from the 96th in 1968. It was a presidential year and while Hubert Humphrey didn't win the presidency, he did well enough in the City of Lancaster to enable me to squeak back in with a plurality of 865 votes. As in 1964, I benefited from the fact that African-American and Hispanic voters, who made up an increasingly important part of the electorate in the City of Lancaster, tended to vote more heavily in presidential years.

Looking forward to the 1970 election in what was now clearly the most marginal legislative seat in Pennsylvania the local Republican leadership decided to by-pass Mr. Rutherford and to endorse, instead, a fresh face -- Harold Horn, an insurance broker. A possibly decisive event occurred when the Lancaster Housing Authority proposed scattered site public housing in the 8th Ward, a bastion of Irish and German Democratic Catholic votes. My opponent denounced the move and promised to introduce legislation to prevent it; I opined, correctly but somewhat lamely, that it was an affair for the Mayor and City Council, not the legislature. I was legally right and politically wrong. I won the eighth ward by a much smaller plurality than usual and lost the district by 239 votes.

The future looked bleak. I had run five times, winning twice and losing three times. I could perhaps win again, in a presidential year, but I had little appetite for another round of doorbells. It looked as though, at age 40, my political career -- and thus my political education -- was over.

*   *   *

Campaigning for the 96th district was a fairly low-key enterprise in the 1960s. I had primary opposition only once, from a fringe candidate who received fewer than 100 votes. So the real campaigning, as opposed to the planning, didn't begin until the summer. My five legislative campaigns were conducted along similar lines, so I will content myself with a generic description.

The campaign began in February with the circulation and filing of nominating petitions. When I hear people like Ralph Nader (a law school classmate, by the way) fulminating against the two major political parties, I wonder whether they understand the effort that goes into sustaining even a party as feeble as the Democratic Party of Lancaster County. Petitions must be circulated in what is often foul weather. They can be signed only by a person of the same party as the one on whose behalf the petition is being circulated. The signature must correspond to the person's signature on file in the

Court House. Ditto marks may not be used. Various affidavits must be signed by the circulator and the candidate, and notarized. And for all this, there is no reward except winning or the satisfaction of knowing that you have kept the two-party system alive.

No sooner have you filed nominating petitions than you are inundated by questionnaires, a flood which increases with each passing decade. Some are from state-wide organizations like the Chamber of Commerce or the AFL-CIO and raise a wide range of issues. Others focus on much narrower concerns – for example, the deposit of out-of-state trash in Pennsylvania or riverboat gambling. But all demand to be answered promptly.

Whether to answer them, and how, poses some delicate questions. Some questionnaires allow only a "yes" or "no" answer when a more nuanced reply would be more faithful to your own views. Some are phrased in ways that make an honest reply difficult if not impossible. In the beginning, I tended to fill them all out; toward the end I did so only when I thought there was a realistic chance of an endorsement or contribution. What I really wanted to do was to reply to all questionnaires along the following lines:

> I am flattered that you wish to know my view on games of chance. But I am swamped with questionnaires and cannot reply to all of them without taking valuable time away from other segments of the campaign. I will therefore divulge my views on various issues of interest to the citizens of the district at times and places of my own choosing.

How will that play in Peoria? Not very well, I am afraid.

Next comes the recruitment of a campaign committee, which after the primary began meeting weekly for lunch at some local hostelry. It usually included, in addition to myself and John Hartman, Mayor Monaghan; Sid Wise and Dick Schier of the Franklin and Marshall faculty; a student intern if we had one; the finance chairman (in 1968 and 1970 it was Elaine Holden, a registered Republican but a loyal fan of mine); Bob Ibold, a PR type; and two or three others.

Television is largely irrelevant at this level of politics. If I had bought spots on Lancaster's Channel 8 only about 5% of the people seeing them could have voted for me. Radio was less expensive and easier to target, leading us to make selective use of that medium. But mostly it was door-to-door, with occasional appearances before the very small number of civic or fraternal groups willing to provide a platform. Because TV was irrelevant fund-raising was not an all-consuming activity, although my campaign expenditures escalated gradually from about $2000 in 1962 to about $20,000 in 1970.

The issue of how to fund our political system has been the subject of intense debate at least since 1975, when Watergate stimulated the passage of Federal legislation creating the Federal Election Commission and imposing certain limits on campaign contributions and expenditures in federal elections. Some of these limitations were rejected in 1976 by the U.S. Supreme Court as violation of First Amendment rights. One unanticipated outcome was the development of political action committees on a large scale. In 2001 Congress passed, and President George W. Bush reluctantly signed, a bill outlawing so-called "soft money" to candidates but not to parties and issue-related committees. It is too soon to evaluate the long-term effects of this "reform," although it is clearly being undermined by the creation of so-called "527" committees. Campaign finance has been a major issue in the states as well. A number of them, including New Jersey, Arizona, and Maine, have experimented with some form of public subvention of gubernatorial and/or state legislative campaigns. Pennsylvania, true to form, has done nothing in this area; it is one of the few states where there are no limitations on the size of campaign contributions.

Those who argue in favor of campaign finance reform point to several features of the present scene which they deem unhealthy. The recent (2002) gubernatorial campaign in Pennsylvania cost upwards of $60 million; it is hard to believe that those who donated generously to these campaigns do not have expectations of favorable administrative or legislative treatment. Another outcome is the growing number of extremely wealthy persons winning congressional races, i.e., in the Senate Jay Rockefeller and Jon Corzine on the Democratic side, Jack Heinz and Peter Fitzgerald on the Republican side. But which is more of an affront to democracy, a Senator whose private wealth enables him to vote as he pleases or a Senator who is beholden to the so-called "special interests" – labor unions, pharmaceutical manufacturers, trial lawyers, gun owners, tobacco growers, etc.? Another problem with the present system is that as the cost of campaigning continues to rise more rapidly than the inflation index, senators and representatives end up devoting a disproportionate part of their time and energy raising money, often far beyond the boundaries of the state or district they represent.

Opponents of the present reform efforts make several arguments. One is that campaign contributions buy "access" but not "influence." This is nonsense. Anyone who has frequented the legislative scene, whether in Washington or the state capitols, knows that big bucks affect the big decisions. It is true that on a small number of issues of particular salience to the general public – social security, for example, or prescription drugs – an aroused public can dictate the general direction of public policy, although even as to these issues the people who finance campaigns can influence the details (and the devil, as we know all too well, is in the details). But on many of the issues coming before Congress and the state legislatures there is no effective public opinion that needs to be respected; members are free to vote their consciences or, lacking a conscience, their pocketbooks.

Another argument against current reform efforts is that, unless the Supreme Court has a change of heart, some of them are likely to be found unconstitutional. (One notes in passing, though it does not invalidate the argument, that many opponents of campaign finance reform are not, in other contexts, noted for their devotion to the First Amendment). But there are indications in recent Supreme Court opinions that some members of the Court may be willing to rethink this issue, so the question of constitutionality may not be moot.

My own point of view diverges from both those I have just described; I am for reform but think attempts to limit contributions and expenditures are probably unworkable. We live in a capitalist society. It is a democratic form of capitalism, to be sure (are democracy and capitalism mutually reinforcing, as Schumpeter thought, or incompatible?), but it is capitalism nonetheless. In a capitalist society money counts, except in those rapidly shrinking areas which are still governed either by custom or strongly held ethical or religious convictions. When Congress is making decisions that are worth billions of dollars to corporations and individuals – whether to develop a new fighter plane or to allow the Food and Drug Administration to regulate tobacco as a narcotic – it is inevitable that the corporations and individuals who have contributed generously will seek to influence the outcomes. As the case of political action committees has already shown and the proliferation of the so-called Section 527 committees emphasizes, if you cut off one channel the river of money will carve out another channel in remarkably quick time.

My own program for reform has three elements. First, I would strengthen disclosure requirements, although the effectiveness of such a step requires a press willing to dig and a public willing to read. Second, I would go as far as the Supreme Court will allow in limiting paid political advertising on television, which in many campaigns accounts for at least 50% of the total campaign budget. And finally – and most importantly – I would press for some modest form of public subvention of campaign costs.

If Pennsylvania were to enact a law that for each dollar raised privately, up to $25,000, a candidate for the Pennsylvania House could receive $2 in matching funds, it would give every candidate who raises the threshold amount a nest egg of $75,000. A candidate could choose to opt out of the system, as Bush, Dean and Kerry opted out of the primaries in the federal system in 2004. Some incumbents might choose to participate in such a program; where they do, we have obviously created a level playing field. But even where the incumbent chooses to rely solely on private contributions, as a majority would doubtlessly do, the situation of the challenger is much improved. Raising $25,000 should not be beyond the powers of a serious challenger, and the resulting $75,000 budget would make possible at least a minimally effective campaign, probably not a winning campaign (although there is always the possibility that a candidate or an issue will "catch fire") but one that will attract attention.

In the end, I am pessimistic about the possibility of doing much to lessen the impact of money on American politics. Too much is at stake, both for those who seek to influence the allocation of public monies and for those who make the allocations. I was once told by a prominent Democratic member of Congress that he was opposed to merging two federal educational programs because it would cut back two sources of campaign contributions to one! To a significant degree we are now more accurately described as a plutocracy rather than a democracy.

* * *

In Lancaster I began ringing doorbells out of necessity: apart from press releases and letters to the editor, canvassing was the only form of campaigning that was free. A group of high school and college students, recruited by me, would gather at a designated house on a Saturday morning. Equipped with street lists (the official roster of people registered to vote in a precinct), voter registration forms, and some type of campaign leaflet, we would sally forth. At first we met with some hostility; Republican voters couldn't believe that a Democrat in Lancaster County had the audacity to be out in broad daylight. Doors were slammed in our faces. But gradually, over the years, people became much more cordial; today, even in the very Republican suburb where I now live, we seldom meet with anything worse than, "Aren't you wasting your time?" Invitations to "have a spot of tea" -- and others even more interesting -- have to be turned down in favor of covering as many households as possible.

The general failure of local civic and fraternal groups to offer a platform to aspiring office-seekers continues to puzzle me. Is it the lingering result of a Puritan-fed suspicion of politics in any form? A failure of civic conscience? Or a partisan unwillingness, in a predominantly Republican county, to provide minority candidates with anything like a level playing field? Whatever the reasons, it is creditable to no one.

Press coverage tended to be casual until after Labor Day. Lancaster is one of very few small cities (population, 58,000) with a morning and an evening paper, both owned by the Steinman family, as is the Sunday News. The morning Intelligencer Journal routinely endorses Democratic and the evening New Era, Republican candidates while the Sunday News generally remains neutral. In the eyes of the New Era I was a "tool of the big city bosses." I tended to view the New Era as viciously Republican and the Intelligencer Journal as tepidly Democratic, but I'm sure my Republican opponent had a different perspective.

I tried coffeeklatches, popularized by Jack Kennedy in his 1958 Senate campaign in Massachusetts, but found they didn't work nearly as well in an urban environment and for a decidedly less sexy candidate. I have an especially vivid recollection of a coffee hosted by Pauline Leet, then a Democratic Committeewoman in the Third Precinct of the Fifth Ward, who was mortified when only one neighbor showed up. I explained that it really didn't matter whether there was one or twenty present; in either case, radio stations WGAL and WLAN would give me airtime and the Intelligencer Journal would print my press release, beginning "speaking to a crowd of friends and neighbors at the home of Pauline Leet, 249 College Avenue, John Pittenger..." Pauline was sufficiently mollified that at a later date she consented to become my wife.

Election Day itself was torture, at least the last three times around. The custom in Lancaster is for candidates to visit all 41 polling places, a custom I deplored but felt powerless to abandon. My humor was not improved by the fact that under state law drinks could not be served in restaurants until the polls closed, a most inhumane law, since repealed.

The polls closed at 8 p.m., and party workers began drifting into our basement meeting room, replete with exposed overhead pipes and fading posters of long forgotten campaigns. Returns were posted on a large board especially constructed for the occasion. In 1970, my fifth (and final) race, I was too nervous to mingle with the crowd. Some feckless committeeman was bound to boast of having gotten me more votes in his precinct than the Democratic registration, a hollow claim in a town where many Democrats register as Republicans for social or business reasons; I wasn't sure I could manage a civil reply. So I hid out upstairs, in our daytime office. Shortly after 9 p.m. a glum John Hartman came in to tell me that I'd lost; there were only two precincts outstanding, and they couldn't possibly erase the 200+ vote deficit I was facing. So a decade of campaigning came to a close. It was an especially bitter pill to swallow as I was the only Democratic House incumbent to lose in Pennsylvania that year while Milton Shapp, our candidate for Governor, was carrying the state by half a million votes and pulling in with him a Democratic majority of 110 to 93 in the House.

At about 9:30 I made the ceremonial trip to Republican Headquarters to concede and congratulate Harold Horn, my opponent. It was the hardest two blocks I ever traversed. Yet the custom is an important one, and needs to be sustained. The defeated candidate is acknowledging the legitimacy of the other's victory and the victor is acknowledging, at least implicitly, that his win is not permanent. "The loyal opposition" is not a hackneyed phrase, but honors a fundamental feature of democratic politics. It is the inability to treat the other side as mistaken, but not evil, that makes democracy so fragile in Northern Ireland, the former Yugoslavia, and elsewhere.

I did not, however, regard the sixties as a lost decade. The five campaigns contributed greatly to my political education, and I accomplished some modestly useful things during my two terms in the legislature (see Chapter 5). In my last column for the morning paper I had written, perhaps with a premonition of what was to come, that the real test of a politician was whether he left his constituents better able to judge the true nature of their interests. Judging by that standard, I think I succeeded. One measure of my success lay in the fact that the two representatives who succeeded me in the 96th district, Marvin Miller, Jr., a Republican (1973-1990) and P. Michael Sturla, a Democrat (1991-present) were both able and conscientious spokesmen for the residents of the district.

Chapter 5 - A Member of the House

The state capitol building in Harrisburg is a majestic structure, built in 1906 at a cost vastly inflated by Boies Penrose, then the Republican boss of the state, to replace one that had burned in 1897. The chamber of the House of Representatives is splendiferous, with a high ceiling, magnificent chandeliers and murals, fore and aft, painted by Violet Oakley in the pre-Raphaelite style. But the splendor of the building that housed them was not matched by the other provisions made for members of the General Assembly. In 1964 it was poorly staffed and equipped, even in comparison with other large-state legislatures. Members' offices were their desks on the floor of the House, committee meetings were often held on short notice at the rear of the House, and lobbyists roamed the floor. I had at that stage only a textbook knowledge of state legislatures. As a lawyer, I had some reasonably accurate notions about the legislative process and the interpretation of statutes, thanks largely to a course at Harvard Law School, "The American Legal System" taught by Dean Albert Sachs. Otherwise, I thought it simply a matter of reading bills and voting for the good ones and against the bad ones.

I had consulted Otis V. Morse IV, the charming and ebullient Democratic state chairman from York County, before running again in 1964. My question was a simple one: if elected, could I do anything useful since I would be the sole Democrat in the Lancaster County delegation. His answer was equally simple: "Can you read and understand a bill?" In those days the Democratic caucus still harbored a number of fairly dim lights, mostly products of the Philadelphia and Allegheny county organizations; like the members of Parliament described in Iolanthe, they "always voted at their party's call and never thought of thinking for themselves at all." I appreciate those back benchers now more than I did then; today's legislators are more literate but less tractable.

My first term in the House coincided with Governor Scranton's last two years in office. William Warren Scranton was one of a now nearly extinct species, a moderate Republican. He hailed from Scranton, a small city whose fortunes had been entangled with his family's for several generations. Tall and good-looking with a quizzical smile generally illuminating his face, he was an ideal candidate for statewide office, and had easily defeated Richardson Dilworth, the reform Democratic Mayor of Philadelphia, for governor in 1962. In office he put together a first-rate staff, one he could have taken to the White House if the occasion had arisen. He worked as easily with the Democratic House majority in the 1965-66 session as he had with the Republican House majority in the 1963-64 session; in fact, he described the former as "surprisingly productive and progressive." His tragedy was that the Pennsylvania Constitution then limited governors to one term, and his somewhat quixotic run at Goldwater for the 1964 Republican presidential nomination was a classic case of too little and too late.

The Johnson landslide in 1964 had produced a House Democratic majority of 116-93, the largest in many years. Herb Fineman later told me he didn't like such handsome majorities because they tended to encourage members to stray from the reservation. We elected as Speaker a senior but otherwise obscure member from Beaver County, on the theory (apparently) that his presence in the chair would deflect Republican criticism about the "city bosses." It didn't work.

Our caucus nominated as Majority Leader Joshua Eilberg of Philadelphia, a lawyer and later a Congressman. Republicans spread the rumor, unsubstantiated as far as I was concerned, that the telephone on his desk was a direct line to Frank Smith, the Democratic boss of Philadelphia, from whom he supposedly took his orders. Herb Fineman became Majority Whip and as Caucus Chairman we installed K. Leroy Irvis, an African-American legislator from the Hill district in Pittsburgh, an area made vivid to many Americans through the novels of John Wideman and the plays of August Wilson. Leroy was a wise and delightful colleague; though he had suffered at the hands of Jim Crow, he was not bitter. Speaking from the microphone near his desk one day I looked down to see him reading from the Book of Jeremiah. Later, when I teased him about not paying close attention to my inspired words, he said, morosely, "I'm just reminding myself that the human race has always been this way."

As in Congress, floor debate does not occupy a great deal of the legislature's time nor does it often influence the fate of the bill under consideration. I can think of only one instance in which anything I said on the floor of the House made even a small contribution to the outcome. The occasion was a debate on reapportionment, set in motion by Supreme Court decisions in the early sixties decreeing "one person, one vote" – i.e., legislative districts had to be equal in population, a test which Pennsylvania could not then meet because under our state constitution each county had to have at least one representative. Part of the problem was a crazy-quilt of single-member and multiple-member districts. Lancaster County, for example, had a single-member seat (my own) and a three-member seat containing the rest of the county. Neighboring York County, with roughly the same population and demographic characteristics, consisted of four single-member seats. The purpose was evident: to insulate Lancaster County from any Democratic inroads outside the City of Lancaster while at the same time allowing Republicans to pick off one or more of the rural York County seats, then mostly held by Democrats.

Strictly speaking, multiple-member seats did not violate the Court's edicts if the population figures were correct. But the Democratic leadership of the House asked me to research the matter, and in doing so I came across a Supreme Court case in which the issue was whether multiple-member seats in the Georgia Senate violated the "one person, one vote" principle. The Court concluded that it did not, subject to the important caveat that any hint of racial gerrymandering, i.e., using multiple-member seats to diminish African-American influence, would be looked at with a jaundiced eye. In a speech on the floor, I warned the Republican minority that we would treat any attempt to preserve multiple-member seats as a civil rights issue. I trust that my comments helped persuade them not to try to perpetuate a mix of single-member and multiple-member seats (this was at a time when Republicans were making at least half-hearted efforts to woo African-American voters).

I was assigned to two standing committees – Ways and Means and Third Class Cities. Neither had much by way of an agenda; in fact, the whole point of Ways and Means was to keep tax measures off the House's agenda. Tommy Frascella, an excitable Philadelphian with a raspy voice, chaired the committee. Tommy accosted me one day: "Hey, Pittenger, I got a job for you." It seems that a nascent statewide organization of college students had persuaded one of my colleagues to introduce a bill repealing the state sales tax on college textbooks. This was said to be hugely popular on the campuses, and the students had extracted a promise from our leadership that we would hold a public hearing on the bill. Would I conduct the hearing, aided by a couple of my colleagues? I would, and did.

The students gave a glowing account of the virtues of their bill. Then I began to question them. How much, I asked the young man who was leading the delegation, did he spend each semester on textbooks? About $60. At the current rate of 6%, how much did the tax add to the cost of his purchase? $3.60. Was this a serious hardship? Well, perhaps not for him, but for others. How much would the bill, if enacted, cost the Commonwealth in reduced sales tax revenue? He hadn't a clue. [The Sales Tax Bureau of the Department of Revenue had given me an estimate of $1.8 million]. Wouldn't that amount of money be better spent awarding scholarships to genuinely needy students rather than giving $3.60 to each student? The subcommittee voted unanimously not to report the bill to the floor, and the issue went away.

The Committee on Third Class Cities, chaired by an Allegheny County legislator, mostly busied itself with police and fire pensions. Looking back, I see that I had no vision about how cities could be helped by the General Assembly, either directly, through subsidized housing, or indirectly, by removing some of the obstacles to annexation, and regret the missed opportunities to help Lancaster and the other smaller cities.

I was, however, deeply involved in several other issues beyond the jurisdiction of my assigned committees. One was student aid. Governor Scranton had signed into law in the 1963-64 session a bill creating the Pennsylvania Higher Education Assistance Agency (PHEAA) and authorizing it to guarantee bank loans to Pennsylvania undergraduates. We Democrats were determined to graft a scholarship program onto that legislation. Governor Scranton was not opposed in principle, but wanted the cost kept down. As I recall, we compromised on $4 million in the first year. I helped Jim Gallagher, chairman of the House Education Committee, draft the bill. It was short and sweet: financial need was the only criterion and the program was to be administered by PHEAA, not by the Department of Education, whose bureaucracy we mistrusted (ironically, in view of my later career).

In one sense our joint scholarship and loan program has been a roaring success. In the most recent year for which I have figures the state disbursed $325 million in direct scholarships and had guaranteed $48 billion in outstanding loans. It is widely viewed as one of the most successful state programs of its kind. When Congress created the Pell grants in 1972, they tried, without success, to hire PHEAA's director to run their program, which was beset by administrative problems for the first several years of its existence.

But in another sense the PHEAA scholarship program illustrates an enduring weakness in our democracy. I had wanted a program that focused on the most needy students, defraying a substantial part of their college costs. But my colleagues rejected this approach as "elitist;" they wanted to spread the money around. For fairly obvious reasons they much preferred 1,000 grants of $1,000 each to 100 grants of $10,000 each, and this has continued to be the pattern. As a result, college-going continues to be heavily influenced by family income, especially since the grants, like the Pell grants from Congress, have grown much less rapidly than the rate of inflation in college costs.

Our democracy does a good job of making educational resources broadly available, the GI bill being perhaps the best example. But sometimes a problem is localized in a particular area or a particular segment of the population. In those circumstances, how do we persuade legislators to vote for expenditures that will not benefit their own constituents directly? The best answer I have been able to devise is to talk in terms of long-term as opposed to short-term benefits. But there is no use complaining about the fact that legislators prefer their own constituents. They are, after all, in the business of getting re-elected; if they are seen to vote in ways that are inimical to current local interests, they will be voted out. The best we can hope for, in a democracy, is some improvement at the margins.

One postscript to the scholarship legislation: As Secretary of Education I was later an ex-officio member of the PHEAA Board. One day our agenda included the interesting case of a young African-American who as a teenager had been convicted of murder and sentenced as a juvenile to an indefinite term of confinement. While in prison he took correspondence courses, earned a General Equivalency Diploma, and then an associate degree. Now in his late twenties, and about to be paroled, he had applied to PHEAA for student aid to finish his baccalaureate degree.

Although the prisoner's behavior during his confinement had been impeccable one of my colleagues, a Republican from suburban Harrisburg, argued that an award in these circumstances would amount to an "endorsement of crime." The debate was hot and heavy, but with the votes of all four non-legislators on the Board, and some discreet lobbying by staff, who were supportive, we voted to approve the application. I look back on that incident as one of my few unqualified bureaucratic triumphs.

Much of my time in my second term was devoted to chairing an ad hoc committee on the thorny subject of exemptions from the local school and municipal property taxes. Under Pennsylvania law churches, hospitals, schools and colleges, and government buildings are tax exempt so long as profit-making activities do not take place on their premises. The problem lay not with the exemptions themselves -- few legislators would be so foolhardy as to advocate repeal of the exemption of church-owned property, for example -- but with the way they are distributed. In suburban and rural areas, exempt property seldom reaches 10% of total market value in the municipality, and often falls below 5%. In some cities, however, as much as 25% of the total value of real property is exempt from taxation for one reason or another. And although people who live outside the city use the city hospitals, colleges, government buildings, and museums, the burden of their being tax-exempt falls entirely on non-exempt property owners in the city. The resulting higher levels of taxation in the cities drive taxpayers out to the suburbs further weakening an already precarious tax base, with especially grave consequences for city school districts.

Our ad hoc committee held hearings around the state, pondered the questions raised, and issued a report which I mostly wrote. Our central recommendation was to create a fund at the state level - we talked about $30 million - from which the state would reimburse municipalities which were losing more than a certain percentage of their property tax revenues because of exemptions. The revenue arithmetic was fairly easy; the political arithmetic was daunting. Urban legislators whose districts stood to gain from such a law were already a distinct minority, and losing influence with each decennial reapportionment; suburban legislators, growing steadily in numbers, had no motive, other than Christian charity (always in short supply) to be supportive. The bill we crafted to carry out our recommendations never reached the floor of the House. The problem is, if anything, more acute in 2004 than it was 35 years ago, as I discovered recently when I chaired a group studying the finances of the School District of Lancaster. We found that tax-exempt property was 20% of the tax base in the city district but no higher than 13% in any of the suburban or rural districts. As a result, city school taxes were 17 mills while the highest rate in any of the affluent suburbs was about 13 mills. There is still nothing approaching a majority in our legislature for a fair system of school finance, as Governor Rendell has discovered.

By my second term, the conditions of legislative life had improved somewhat. In the 1969-1970 session I shared an office and a secretary with four Democratic colleagues from western Pennsylvania – Gil DeMedio, John Laudadio, Jim Manderino and Denny Bixler. They all had their good points -- Laudadio had pioneered the Clean Streams Act of 1959, and Manderino eventually rose to become Speaker before succumbing to a heart attack at much too early an age – but although we were all Democrats, we hardly spoke the same language, so different were the political cultures from which we had emerged.

One morning DeMedio asked if I would trade him five Game Codes for five Fish Codes (these were summaries of state law and regulations relating to hunting and fishing, respectively, and were very popular with the sportsmen among our constituents). A trade was arranged. Five minutes later, he was back: did I know a certain Justice of the Peace in northern Lancaster County? One of his constituents had been arrested for speeding on the Pennsylvania

Turnpike, and the question was how "reasonable" the local Justice of the Peace could be expected to be.

This time I exploded in righteous wrath: "Gil, dammit, all you ever worry about is your constituents and their petty problems. You haven't a clue what we are voting on most of the time." This was not only rude, but, as applied to Gil, untrue. DeMedio should have clocked me. Instead, he smiled and said: "Pitt, you just don't understand the politics of Washington County. Being elected to the legislature out there is like winning the Buick at the Firemen's' Carnival. YOU GOTTA TAKE YOUR FRIENDS AND RELATIONS FOR A RIDE." Gil was trying to teach me something that political scientists have known for a long time, i.e., that political cultures vary from one place to another. In that as in other respects, I was a slow learner. One of the glories of the House Democratic caucus was its diversity; nearly every race and ethnic group in Pennsylvania was represented. The Republican caucus was far more homogenous (less so today). So we had much to learn from each other.

Another illustration of the differences in political cultures concerned constituent mail. Most of my colleagues were inundated with it; I was not. Citizens of Lancaster County describe themselves as self-reliant, and by and large they are. They generally turn to government only in times of real distress. I was grateful not to have to devote an inordinate amount of time to answering the mail, which freed me up to devote more energy to the policy questions that intrigued me. But I probably would have been better off encouraging my constituents to bring their problems to me; it would have helped me consolidate a political base that was at best precarious.

Only on one occasion was my House mailbox filled to overflowing. The Reverend Carl McIntyre, a fundamentalist preacher based in Collingswood, New Jersey, made some anti-Semitic remarks on his gospel radio station. Speaker Fineman, himself Jewish, was outraged and drafted a resolution asking the Federal Communications Commission to investigate with a view toward suspending or revoking McIntyre's broadcasting license. I signed the resolution at Fineman's request, and all hell broke loose; my mailbox was filled each day for two weeks with vitriolic letters and postcards from all over the United States denouncing me as a tool of Satan, etc. One postcard came from a Pittenger in Florida who said I had disgraced the family name. I showed the postcard to my father, who replied: "That's Cousin Fred; he's been a lush for thirty years."

One of my best methods of communicating with my more literate constituents was the morning Lancaster newspaper, the Intelligencer Journal. Harry Stacks, its editor, had suggested that I write a weekly column about events in Harrisburg during the 1965-66 term, and I readily agreed. The writing was not a chore – I sometimes got the first draft done at my desk on the floor of the House – and I tried to keep the columns relatively non-partisan. Probably my best-remembered column was written after a weekend snowstorm which required me to hike about six miles from the farm to the village of Wakefield where I spent the night with a hospitable Mennonite family. During my hike I was frequently encouraged by snowbound householders, one of whom offered me a nip of his best Scotch. I wrote about his hospitality in my column, which earned the poor man a denunciation from the pulpit the following Sunday.

Looking back I'm uncertain about the ethics of a legislator being given free space in a newspaper on a regular basis. The editor tried to deflect possible criticism by cutting me off after the primary when I had been nominated for re-election, and had thus become an active candidate. Perhaps it is simply another one of those advantages that accrue to incumbents,like the mailing of a newsletter or the use of a TV studio in the Capitol. But we need to concern ourselves about the extent to which incumbents are acquiring privileges which make them more or less impregnable (all except me, that is).

One of my more successful ventures during the '69-'70 session was persuading Leroy Irvis, by then the Majority Leader, to allow me to bring one page each week to Harrisburg from my district, including the first woman page in the history of the House. Our regular pages were students at the Harrisburg Area Community College who attended morning classes at the College, showing up at the House about 1 p.m. in time for formal sessions. One of them, John Plebani, later transferred to Franklin and Marshall, with my encouragement, and went on to a distinguished career as a congressional staffer in Washington and then a lobbyist with one of the big K Street lobbying firms.

To avoid controversy I entrusted the selection of pages to the social studies faculties of J.P. McCaskey, our city public high school, and Lancaster Catholic High School, which served the whole county. Each page served only one week, which as a practical matter meant anywhere from one to three days. I greatly enjoyed our conversations driving back and forth to Harrisburg, and still meet ex-pages, now in their early fifties, who tell me that it was a formative experience. I had to watch out, though; one of them drafted a press release for me about the page program which described their duties as "serving the needs of the members of the House both on and off the floor." We decided that sentence had to go.

The 1964 election, in addition to giving Democrats a solid House majority, had swept into office some people who were outside the mold -- products neither of the big city machines nor of the labor unions – steel, auto, and coal – with close ties to the Democratic Party. A group of us freshmen got in the habit of meeting every Monday for lunch, to go over the House calendar and trade information about pending bills. The original members included Paul Hoh, a Lutheran minister from Reading; Kent Shelhamer, a peach and apple grower from Columbia County; and several attorneys in addition to myself – Bob Wise of Williamsport, Jane Alexander from York County, and Bill Eckensberger from Lehigh County. Others joined later. We were careful to keep Eilberg informed about what we were doing, since we did not want to be seen as insurrectionary. He was suspicious but not obstructive. The pressroom dubbed us the "Mushroom Club," it being said about us that the leadership "keeps them in the dark, feeds them shit and hopes they'll grow." If we had ever tried to withhold our votes as a bloc on some issue I suspect the leadership would have cracked down pretty hard, but we never went that far.

Party caucuses played a major role in the life of the House during the '60s, much to the consternation of the press. They were frequent and sometimes lengthy, being used both to inform the troops and to hammer out party positions on major legislation. Discipline was strict but not blind; it was understood that you could go "off the reservation" as a matter of personal conscience or if the nature of your district demanded it.

I benefited from at least one such invocation of caucus discipline. I had introduced a bill to amend the Sales and Use Tax Act which was designed to assist the Donnelley Corporation in locating a new printing plant in Lancaster. Under the rules of the House any other amendment to the Sales Tax was considered "germane" to my bill and thus could have been offered as an amendment. A number of my colleagues were waiting in the wings to offer such amendments which, if accepted, would have doomed my bill because of the loss of revenue to the state. In caucus, Eilberg explained the situation, pointing out that I was the first Democrat from Lancaster County in a long time and demanding to know, "Is any S.O.B. going to offer an amendment?" Silence. So my bill sailed through the House (but was buried in the Republican Senate).

I had several run-ins with Eilberg. One day I was accosted on the floor of the House by J.P. O'Donnell, an amiable organization Democrat from southwest Philadelphia, who was hawking a constitutional amendment to limit the number of lawyers in the

House. Would I sign on as a co-sponsor? I would, and did, and was promptly called into the Majority Leader's office where I was described as a "disgrace to my profession." Although the number is shrinking, there are still (in my judgment) too many lawyers in the legislature and too few from other walks of life. More scientists, for example, would help the House evaluate risks to health and the environment more sensibly than it now does.

On another occasion I went to see Eilberg about a bill co-sponsored by the whole Lancaster County delegation. The Olmsted Air Base just south of Harrisburg was being abandoned by the Air Force, and the plan was to claim part of it for a branch campus of Penn State. With Democrats in the majority and as the only Democrat in the county delegation, I was responsible for seeing the bill safely through the House; the failure to do so would be a distinct embarrassment "back home." When the bill appeared stalled, I went to see Eilberg. His explanation was that he "didn't want any damn college professors within 50 miles of Harrisburg." I pointed out that professors at Elizabethtown, Millersville, Franklin and Marshall, Dickinson, Shippensburg, Lebanon Valley and Susquehanna among others were already within the magic orbit; eventually he relented.

The Pennsylvania legislature, like New York's, has always been dominated by its leadership, with rank and file members having relatively little to say about major decisions, especially those involving budget and taxes. Conference committees must be appointed after the two houses have passed differing versions of a bill. Under Pennsylvania rules a conference committee consisted of two majority and one minority member from each house, or six in all, and the conference report had to be signed by four conferees, including at least two from each house. Often budget amendments that had been passed by the full House were flushed down the drain by the conference committee; the final budget was negotiated between the leaders of the majority party in each house and the governor, and then presented on a take-it-or-leave-it basis to both houses. Efficient, but highly undemocratic.

Lobbyists were ubiquitous – and, for the most part, helpful. They were often a quicker and more reliable source of information than state government itself. For example, when we were considering amendments to the state public school subsidy system, the teachers union would be hours and sometimes days ahead of the Department of Education in furnishing printouts showing the impact of the proposed changes in all 203 House districts. But computers can be a curse as well as a blessing; the prompt availability of detailed information leaves House members less room to maneuver, winners and losers being all too evident. Perhaps we were better off in the old days when debate focused more on principles and less on printouts.

I remember only one occasion on which a lobbyist went too far. It was in connection with some minor revision to the state liquor code. The lobbyist in question poked his forefinger at my necktie and threatened me with dire consequences if I failed to support his position. I told him to get lost, and suffered no retribution.

One's colleagues could sometimes be more overbearing than any lobbyist. One such was Martin Mullen, a staunch Catholic from

West Philadelphia who was rumored to have the ear of Cardinal Krol. Marty approached me about supporting a bill expanding state aid to private schools. He ended up threatening to come into Lancaster and get every Catholic in my district to vote against me. I fully intended to support the bill (35 years later I am less clear about its wisdom) but I resented his heavy-handedness. I told him I'd welcome his presence and predicted I would get over half the Catholic vote. He retreated.

I spoke in Chapter 2 about media coverage of local politics, which I described in somewhat unflattering terms. But the coverage of state government and politics is worse, and has been deteriorating for several decades. Forty years ago most of the major metropolitan dailies had Harrisburg bureaus staffed by several fulltime reporters and some of them, like Duke Kaminski of the Philadelphia Bulletin, stayed around long enough to acquire some genuine expertise. Nowadays the bureaus are smaller and the reporters tend to stay for shorter periods of time. As a result, they are seldom able to get below the surface of things in any meaningful way.

One issue that the press excels in raising, if not in clarifying, is that of "conflict of interest." No sensible person would quarrel with the proposition that a legislator should not vote on a bill from which he would derive direct personal pecuniary benefit – for example, a bill authorizing the Commonwealth to buy land owned by the legislator for incorporation into a state park. But what is "direct"? Suppose a bill benefits a legislator as one of a class, the most common being a member of a profession or occupation; must he refrain from voting in those circumstances? Does it make any difference whether the class has a membership of 10 or 10,000? And how direct must the benefit be? I was once consulted by an eminent Philadelphia lawyer about whether a member of City Council could properly vote to raise the pensions of city firefighters if his brother was a retired fireman. I said "yes" but he advised his client to the contrary.

It seems to me that the whole conflict of interest notion has been pushed far beyond its useful limits. That is the gist of a very good article by Bayliss Manning, entitled "The Purity Potlatch." Potlatch is a term used by anthropologists to describe the custom prevalent among some Esquimaux tribes where merit derives from giving gifts to others more substantial than the ones you have received. Tribes have been known to destroy themselves through this competitive gift-giving. Something similar seems to be going on in the modern political world. Candidate A announces she will make public her income tax returns for the previous year. Candidate B responds by making public his returns for the past five years. Candidate A ups the ante by including her husband's returns. Candidate B counters by including parents and children, and so on. All this is reported breathtakingly by the press while more substantive issues are ignored.

The press infatuation with conflict of interest probably has two sources. One is that moral issues are deemed to be intrinsically more newsworthy than policy issues; describing Congressman X as being guilty of a conflict of interest is page one stuff, while describing as unwise the policies embedded in his bill to regulate public utility accounting practices gets relegated to page 14. The other reason is the understaffing of state house news offices; the conflict of interest claim doesn't ordinarily require the sort of research that the regulation of public utility accounting practices demands, so it gets priority.

My own policy as a legislator was to avoid both palpable conflicts and the appearance of conflict. For example, the Philadelphia Phillies sent complimentary tickets to members of the House and Senate in the spring of each year. As an ardent Phillies fan, it was with real reluctance that I returned mine with a polite note expressing my chagrin at not being able to take advantage of their generosity. When a story to this effect hit the papers some of my colleagues were not too happy with my "showing them up" as they put it. In answer to their queries I was hard-pressed to suggest issues on which a legislator's vote could have been influenced by free baseball tickets. The only one I could think of at the time was an obscure state law, later repealed, which forbade professional baseball teams from starting an inning after 6 p.m. on Sunday – an attempt, I suppose, to eliminate competition with Sunday evening church services.

But recent developments have made it evident that the fate of the Phillies is in fact closely intertwined with state legislative policy, making my self-denying ordinance seem less quixotic. In 2000 Governor Ridge proposed issuing state bonds in the amount of $320 million to defray part of the cost of new stadia for the Phillies, Eagles, Pirates, and Steelers. (The fact that Ridge was doing this at the same time he was refusing additional financial help to

Philadelphia and other urban school districts sheds an interesting light on his priorities; perhaps the explanation is that millionaire owners of professional sports franchises contribute, often generously, to political campaigns, while the parents of poor kids don't). At any rate, the bill passed; and the fact that $10 million has been allocated to Lancaster County for a baseball stadium doesn't mollify me in the least.

If I have been harsh in some of my judgments about members of the press, I can at least exonerate them from one charge, that of misquoting politicians. In my forty-five years in public life I can't recall a single instance of being misquoted, that is, reported as having said something that I did not in fact say. Sometimes a reporter has taken a statement of mine and emphasized a minor point to the neglect of my central message, or drawn unwarranted conclusions from what I have said; but neither of these practices deserves the opprobrium attaching to an outright misquotation. So when a politician says he has been misquoted, I am skeptical; the ritual claim that he was "quoted out of context" is, in most cases, shorthand for, "My God, I wish I hadn't said that."

So why does the press pay so little attention to state government?

Some of the blame can be laid at the foot of the Jacksonians, who in the decades after the War of 1812 made sure that most state capitols – Augusta, Montpellier, Trenton, Harrisburg, Annapolis, etc. – would be in the boondocks away from the evil influences of the big cities (and, not incidentally, away from the scrutiny of the metropolitan newspapers). But the latter are not free from blame. In Pennsylvania the metropolitan dailies -- the Inquirer, the Daily News, and the now-defunct Bulletin in Philadelphia, the Post Gazette and the now defunct Press in Pittsburgh -- have consistently regarded Harrisburg as a prelude to assignment to City Hall, a sort of Triple AAA league in which reporters were seasoned for three or four years before being promoted to the majors.

Liberals have something to answer for as well. Beginning with the New Deal, they have seen Washington as the solution to one problem after another. Many assumed either that the states would fade into oblivion or that they would become mere administrative arms of the national government. As a result, few political scientists paid much attention to what the states were doing. But they survived; and in an era when the Supreme Court is beginning to show some willingness to revive the interstate commerce clause as a restriction on national power, and skepticism is growing about Washington's ability to solve everything, more attention is surely due the states. But I don't see it happening yet.

My fellow citizens must shoulder some responsibility for the relative neglect of state government. A federal system is not easy to understand; if air or water pollution is a problem, disentangling the roles of national, state, and local governments is sometimes a tough job. Most people would rather not bother. Washington makes dramatic decisions about war and peace, unemployment and inflation, and City Hall is just a stone's throw away. Everything in between is a blur.

One might think that Congress would be respectful of the states and their rightful role in a federal system. After all, Congress is full of former governors and state legislators, many of whom campaigned for national office on platforms urging the return of power to the states. But once they arrived in Washington they saw things a little differently. As my friend Alan Rosenthal is fond of saying, "where you stand depends on where you sit," or, as Justice O'Connor put it in a recent case, the Courts cannot rely on Congress' "underdeveloped capacity for self-restraint." And so we have the spectacle of self-described conservative members of Congress voting repeatedly to nationalize power at the expense of the states – for example, by giving the federal courts jurisdiction over crimes once the exclusive province of state law, or voting for George W. Bush's "Leave No Child Behind" Act, the most intrusive federal excursion into educational policy in our nation's history.

At one point I debated trying to remedy the neglect of Pennsylvania's state government by the press all by myself. Congressional Quarterly, (CQ), an offshoot of the St. Petersburg (Florida) Times, covers Congress on a weekly basis and has been both a journalistic and a financial success, stimulating a host of other publications. CQ has had several state emulators, the most successful being a bi-weekly journal called the California Reporter, which combines political gossip with solid coverage of state government. I flew to Sacramento once with the idea of determining for myself whether such a venture could succeed in Pennsylvania. We will never know the answer because I was soon distracted by other possibilities.

In any case, I doubt that I had either the journalistic skills or the financial resources needed to succeed in such a venture.

Sometimes the negligence of the press had benign outcomes. During a poorly attended morning session of the House, a Democratic member who was vice-chairman of a major standing committee, in answer to a question from a Republican colleague, made an oblique reference to the drinking habits of his chairman. In fact, the chairman had been "on the wagon" for months if not years. I was incensed. But since the press seemed to have taken no notice of the remark, I thought it unwise to make an issue of it on the floor. Instead, when we adjourned for a caucus later in the day, several of us raised cain, demanding from the offending member an apology which was eventually forthcoming. In dealing with the matter this way we sought to uphold the dignity of the House without highlighting for the press the alleged conduct of the chairman. Others might want to "let it all hang out," but that was not my style.

But my own conduct in this area was not above reproach. In 1969 the Board of Trustees of Millersville State College (now Millersville University) fired President Robert Christie, who was popular with students but not with older faculty and alumni (among his sins -- serving liquor in the President's House). When pressed for an explanation, members of the Board of Trustees declined to go beyond saying that irreconcilable differences had arisen between the President and the Board. One member of the Board was a Republican legislator from a neighboring county. I thought it would be clever to nail him on the floor of the House, where he could not so easily resist demands for an explanation. But I went too far; and Lee Donaldson, the able and decent Republican floor leader, chastised me as being "out of order," which I surely was. The irony is that some years later the same situation arose, except this time it was I, as Secretary of Education, who fired a state college president, and when pressed for reasons, proceeded (unwisely) to discuss them in some detail. The president later sued the Commonwealth, and it cost the taxpayers a considerable sum of money to settle the matter: a classic case of my having learned nothing over the intervening years.

As part of a wider movement to improve its efficiency, the General Assembly, in 1969, created a Joint Legislative Data Processing Committee to explore how computers could be made to serve our needs. Since I was then (and continue to be) computer illiterate, I was somewhat taken aback when Speaker Fineman asked me to chair the committee. His explanation: "You're the only college professor on our side of the aisle." But I was far from being the least sophisticated member of the committee. One of my Senate colleagues, a former professional basketball player, said one day, "Ask the computer what to put in the budget." I explained to him gently – I knew at least this much – that you could only get out of a computer what you had put in by way of data and assumptions. He was greatly disappointed.

A competent executive director and staff compensated for the ignorance of the Joint Committee, and we made considerable progress in computerizing the proceedings of the Senate and House as well as election returns and other useful data. My only disappointment was that having created this very useful research tool, the General Assembly proceeded to cut its utility in half by putting difficulties in the way of journalists and citizens who wanted to have access (for example) to roll call votes. But this is only another illustration of the general rule: any innovation in politics will be absorbed in ways that buttress rather than weaken the status quo.

Because state legislators are not held in very high esteem, in Pennsylvania as elsewhere, I want to conclude this chapter on my legislative service by recounting an instance of political courage which occurred later, but has continued to inspire me; if there were a Pennsylvania volume of "Profiles in Courage" this incident would surely rate a chapter.

Marvin Miller, Sr. was a former newspaperman who served several terms in the Pennsylvania House as a Republican from the multi-member seat in suburban and rural Lancaster County. The 1974 election had resulted in a House with a large Democratic majority. Everyone assumed that Herb Fineman, the Philadelphia lawyer who had been an effective minority leader in the previous session, would be elected Speaker. But they reckoned without Marty Mullen who cordially disliked Fineman. Mullen plotted with a small number of other anti-Fineman Democrats to break ranks: after the Democratic caucus had nominated Fineman, Mullen and his co-conspirators would vote for Ken Lee, the Republican leader, for Speaker, thus giving him a narrow victory, and turning the Republican status from minority to majority.

Miller got wind of the conspiracy, and decided to do something about it. He said publicly that since Democrats were clearly the House majority, they were entitled to a Speaker from their own ranks, even if that person was not the unanimous choice of the Democratic caucus. To do otherwise, Miller maintained, would thwart the will of the majority and thus would be, in some sense, both undemocratic and unconstitutional. Accordingly, when Fineman was nominated and fourteen Democrats defected, Miller and nine like-minded Republicans voted for Fineman, electing him and vindicating the November decision of the electorate. That act of political courage won Miller the undying enmity of many Republicans, and doubtless hastened the end of his political career. When I went to the viewing for Marvin Sr. in the Moravian Church in Lititz several years ago, I wondered how many in the long line of mourners remembered him for that singular act of political courage.

Legislatures are strange beasts. Bismarck is supposed to have said that there are two things you should never see being made – laws and sausages. From the outside legislatures look slow, inefficient and chaotic. Six months after he had defeated me in 1970 Harold Horn stopped me in the basement of the Capitol: "how did you stand it?" he inquired. "We come into session at 11 a.m.; the Chaplain prays; nothing happens for a half hour; the speaker refers a few bills to committee, then declares a recess for lunch. When we return it is to vote on a resolution honoring Maisie Esbenshade, second grade teacher for 42 years in the Smithtown Elementary School; then caucus, which lasts over an hour; then a vote on a bill to raise the fees of constables in counties of the fourth class; then adjourn for the day." Not long after this tirade Harold announced, not surprisingly, that he would not seek a second term.

Legislatures are inefficient. But they are responding to pressures from many sources: constituents, leadership, colleagues, lobbyists, parties, and contributors, as well as to their own more or less deeply held convictions. The result is not pretty, but neither is it to be scorned. The Pennsylvania General Assembly manages to enact a balanced budget each year; to create and sustain a court system that enforces public order and vindicates private rights; to create and fund, however inequitably, a system of free public schools; and to do a host of other things with varying degrees of effectiveness. Looking backward in time, or outward in space, and seeing how badly human beings have managed their affairs in most centuries and most countries, that isn't a contemptible performance, even if it could clearly be improved upon.

We should not be surprised that legislators respond to the "here and now" – to what their constituents want at this moment of history. They are maximizing their chances of being re-elected, which is, after all, their top priority. But we should be clear that in behaving in this self-regarding way they are neglecting dimensions of space and time. The neglect in space (used metaphorically) arises from legislators' unwillingness to pay much attention to persons outside their districts – and persons inside, such as the very poor, criminals, and people not registered to vote – who are perceived to be without influence. The resulting legislation generally favors the status quo:

"To those who have shall it be given, and from those who have not shall it be taken away."

The neglect in time is perhaps, in the long run, even more worrisome, although it has its roots in the same soil – the unborn, like the very poor, cast no votes. But at some point the refusal to look ahead may prove fatal. Our oil reserves are running out; in many parts of the country water is increasingly scarce; scientific developments in genetic engineering threaten major changes in our understanding of what it means to be human. Legislators seem to be only dimly aware of these clouds on the horizon. They will bide their time until it begins to rain – but by that time it may be too late.

Chapter 6 - A Servant of the House

I had been defeated in 1966 in an election in which Ray Shafer, a Republican, became governor, replacing William Scranton, whose lieutenant governor he had been, and Republicans won a 104-99 margin in the Pennsylvania House. The job prospects in Harrisburg for a defeated Democratic legislator were not bright. I was in a generally low frame of mind as I cleared out my desk on the floor of the House and began to think about what lay ahead.

But if I was lethargic, my friends, Sid Wise and Dick Schier, were not. They immediately set about lobbying Herb Fineman, the Philadelphia lawyer who would be Minority Floor Leader after January 1967, on my behalf. After a suspenseful few weeks Fineman offered me a position as Director of Research for the House Democrats. The title was a bit of a misnomer, as I was directing nobody but myself, and the salary, $7500, was ridiculously low. But at that time the minority party disposed of far less staff money than the majority, a defect largely remedied since then, and no one else was beating a path to my door, so I said "yes" and began work in a tiny office on the "E" floor at the rear of the Capitol Building in January of 1967.

My job was to help members of the Democratic caucus with their research needs. I didn't actually draft bills, which was the province of the Legislative Reference Bureau, and I didn't generally write press releases, which was the task of Rusty Cowan in the press office, but I did just about everything else: wrote speeches, researched legislation in other states, kept in touch with what was going on in Congress, sat in on floor sessions and committee hearings, and generally tried to help Fineman keep our wildly ill-assorted and unruly team of Democrats informed and in good spirits.

Some members of the caucus made heavier claims on my time than others. One of the most demanding was Frank Kury, grandson of Polish coal miners, graduate of Trinity College and the University of Pennsylvania Law School. He was bright and persistent – the latter, a quality much under appreciated – and later served with distinction in the state Senate. When he left the General Assembly he had to his credit a series of legislative accomplishments unparalleled in my time: the environmental rights amendment to the state constitution, a parcel of bills reforming the Public Utility Commission, and another parcel spelling out how the Senate should exercise its constitutional power to approve gubernatorial appointments, among others.

Frank came to see me one day about a pet project of his, and as it was his third or fourth visit to my office that week, I lost my cool. "Dammit, Frank," I said, "You must think I am a member of your personal staff. But I'm not -- I work for all 99 of you. I work 50 hours a week, which comes to about 30 minutes per member. By my calculations you have used up all your time until next February. Get lost!" Frank, in some indignation, went to see Fineman, who bawled me out in Frank's presence, but later said, in private, "Look, I know he's a pain in the ass, but he's one our most productive members; do what you can, within reason, to accommodate him." Herb was right, and I did my best (Frank and I are still good friends).

Fineman was a superb leader -- bright, tough and well organized -- although some of the more conservative members of the caucus chafed (privately) under his yoke. One incident will illustrate one of his best qualities -- his willingness to hear the truth, however unflattering. As the House was debating Governor Shafer's budget, Fineman made a long speech attacking the budget and presenting a Democratic alternative. His staff listened on the "squawk box" in his office. After the debate he came bouncing into the office – "Well, boys, how did I do?" The others praised him effusively. "Great speech," "Laid 'em in the aisles," etc. I remained silent. Finally, Herb turned to me – "Pitt, what do you think?" I shrugged: "C minus or D plus." He looked a bit startled. "Why?" "Too long; too many facts and figures; no unifying theme that would give the press a handle." Fineman said to me, quietly, "come see me at 9 a.m. tomorrow." I spent a wakeful night, expecting to be fired, but when I came into his office the next day he merely asked, "What am I paying you?" "$7500." I pointed out that Gene Knopf, my opposite number in the Senate, was making $15,000. So Fineman said, "I'm doubling your salary as of today – you're the only guy who tells me the truth."

If I could ask one and only one question about a politician I was being asked to support, it would be, "does she surround herself with sycophants, or with people who tell her the truth?" The politician who wants to hear only the good news not only shuts herself off from valuable information but also betrays a basic insecurity that will damage her in other ways.

Not only could you tell Fineman the truth, he took staff very seriously, a quality which tended to compensate for low salaries and poor working conditions. I remember a caucus in which he was "rolling the calendar," i.e., reviewing the bills they would be voting on later that day. A secretary came in to tell him about an important phone call. Leaving the caucus to take the call, he turned to me and said, "Pitt, just keep on rolling the calendar." And for a half hour I did just that. Staff at that time were not even allowed into the Republican House caucus, let alone permitted to chair it. Our wider responsibilities gave us a great deal of pride, and cemented our loyalty to Fineman and the rest of the leadership.

One curious episode in the spring of '68 illustrates my somewhat anomalous position on the caucus staff: on the one hand, a lowly staffer, but on the other hand, someone to be reckoned with, politically, at least in a minor way. Pennsylvania was due to elect a State Treasurer and an Auditor-General in the fall of that year. Nominations to those positions often went to party hacks, and some of us younger reform types became restive. I began conversations with Bob Casey, a young Scranton lawyer who had just finished a term in the Senate in 1966. Although endorsed that year for governor by the party, he lost the nomination to Milton Shapp, who in turn lost in November to Shafer. Eventually Casey and I agreed to run for Treasurer and Auditor General as a team, emphasizing our youth and our independence from the big city machines.

But the old-timers were smarter than I thought. They knew that of the two of us Casey posed the far more formidable threat.

So one day I picked up the Harrisburg Patriot to discover that the party leaders were putting together a ticket including Casey for Auditor General and Grace Sloan, a long-time party activist, for State Treasurer. I didn't blame Bob for abandoning our cause, but I thought he might have had the courtesy to let me know personally rather than leaving me to find out from the morning paper. But that did not prevent us from working together in later years.

The General Assembly is far better staffed today than it was in the 60s. There are more staff, they are better qualified, and the two parties have worked out a sensible understanding providing roughly equal amounts of staff money to the majority and minority parties. The Republicans seem to me to have made better use of their staff in one important way: they have kept the hiring in the caucus leadership, resulting in a more cohesive staff operation, whereas the Democrats have delegated much hiring responsibility to committee chairpersons. And a magnificent (and costly) expansion of the Capitol Building in 1987, praised even by the architectural editor of the New York Times, has provided, for the first time, adequate space for both members and staff in the new East Wing.

At the same time, I must confess that these improvements have not, in my judgment, done much to improve the quality of deliberation or of the resulting legislation in the General Assembly. They have put the General Assembly on a more equal footing with the Governor, which is especially important when the governor is of one party and the other party controls one or both houses of the legislature. But they have not done much to fulfill the hopes of those of us who fought for better staffing in order to make the General Assembly a source of thoughtful and well-designed laws.

In assessing this situation, it helps to remember that the top priority of most legislators, Democrat or Republican, liberal or conservative, is being re-elected. If we divide the legislative task into three separate activities – passing laws, overseeing the execution of the laws, and serving the needs of constituents -- it is not hard to guess which gets priority. (Invited once by Jim Manderino, then Majority Leader, to address newly elected legislators before the beginning of a new session, I graded the previous session: A – for constituent service, C+ for legislation, and F for oversight.) Given these priorities, it was inevitable that the bulk of the new resources, staff and facilities, would go into constituent service, no matter what the titles and official responsibilities might be. The flunking grade for legislative oversight is easily explained; the press pays much more attention to an original piece of legislation than to one which "merely" corrects existing statutes. But the result of piling one statute on top of another, without trying to reconcile them, is an increasingly unworkable body of law.

Reapportionment has also affected legislative performance, adversely for the most part. I was among those cheering loudly when the Warren Supreme Court in 1964 handed down its "one person, one vote" edict. It bothered me that while I represented 56,000 people in the 96th district, Admiral Davis, up in Forest County, whose vote counted the same as mine, represented only 6,000. But since the Court's decision came at a time when cities were losing population the principal political effect, at least in Pennsylvania, has been not in altering the balance of power between Republicans and Democrats, but in shifting power within the Republican Party from rural to suburban legislators.

At the same time, the use of computers in the decennial reapportionment has led to wholesale gerrymandering and the further entrenchment of incumbents. The principle governing reapportionment can be easily stated: "We'll strengthen your incumbents if you'll strengthen ours." Each decade fewer and fewer Pennsylvania House seats are contested, as the following chart will show:

Number of House Seats with

Year	No Democratic Candidate, or Democrat getting less than 10%	No Republican Candidate, or Republican getting less than 10%	Total
1950	0	1	1
1960	1	0	1
1970	0	2	2
1980	18	15	33
1990	26	24	50
2000	43	50	93

Reapportionment is not the only culprit, but it is a major one.

Because of these developments, incumbent legislators are close to immune where public opinion is concerned; only a scandal is likely to unseat them. So we are looking at a General Assembly that is increasingly undemocratic both in the mode of its election and in its internal proceedings. In the past only Justice Stevens of the United States Supreme Court seems to have been much concerned about non-racial gerrymandering. My hopes were raised when the Court granted certiorari last year in a Pennsylvania case involving some egregious gerrymandering by Republican majorities in the General Assembly and Governor Ridge, but were promptly dashed this year when a plurality of the Court agreed that partisan gerrymandering might in theory be justiciable, but then proceeded to set the bar so high as to make it unlikely that the Court would ever hold one to be unconstitutional.

Pennsylvania has not succumbed to the lure of term limits as a device for correcting some of the evils noted above; wisely, in my judgment. Although the federal courts have been unanimous in striking down state limitations, constitutional or legislative, on the terms of U.S. Senators and Representatives, federal and state courts have generally allowed state limitations on service in the state legislature to stand. One inevitable result in states such as California has been to shift power from elected legislators to unelected staff, both in the legislature itself and in the executive branch.

Upon entering the General Assembly in 1965 I was convinced, as were many of my colleagues in both parties, that the pendulum had swung too far away from the legislature and toward the governor. Forty years later I wonder whether we have gone too far the other way.

Having been both a member of the legislature and of a Governor's cabinet I fear legislative encroachment on executive power more than gubernatorial encroachment on legislative power. (The Founding Fathers were likewise more concerned about legislative imperialism; hence the creation of a bicameral legislature.) The Governor, after all, is the only person who can speak for the entire state. Legislative concerns are necessarily more parochial. Any major initiative – an overhaul of the tax system, for example, or extensive charges in the laws governing criminal sentencing – is going to require strong leadership from the front office. The legislature can say "aye" or "nay," and can fine-tune the Governor's proposals, but except in rare cases it will not be the nursery of major policy changes.

A development not much commented upon, at least here in Pennsylvania, by the media or the political scientists, is the phenomenon of legislative staff running for the legislature itself. Fifty years ago, when an incumbent legislator retired, his place was generally taken by some local eminence – the Mayor or County Commissioner, an attorney, banker, insurance broker, or prominent farmer. Nowadays anecdotal evidence suggests that the candidate is increasingly likely to have worked for the retiring legislator or for a committee of the General Assembly. After all, the staffer knows the issues and, more important, knows how to organize and finance a campaign, having been deeply involved herself in these activities. The result may be an increase in expertise, but it plays hob with the idea of a citizen legislature; many of these staffers go straight from college onto a legislative payroll without any intervening experience in the private sector. But this is merely another aspect of the increasing professionalization of politics in the United States of America.

My staff experience was a good one. It taught me humility – a useful quality in politicians, provided the dose is small – and enabled me to be a more useful member of the House in my second term. It may well be, in fact, that I missed my calling, and that, rather than aspiring to elective office, I should have pursued a career in the executive branch. Like Coriolanus, I tended to disdain the mob, not a good attribute in one seeking office in a democratic system. But the lure of the candle was too much for this particular moth...

Chapter 7 - The Governor's Man

Readers will recall that we left my political career in a shambles in November 1970, having been defeated as an incumbent for the second time. But I didn't have long to mourn my fate. A half hour after I conceded the phone rang in Democratic Headquarters. It was Governor-elect Milton Shapp. I congratulated him on winning by half a million votes; he commiserated with me on my narrow defeat. What were my plans, he asked? I said, truthfully, that I didn't have any. He made me promise I wouldn't accept a position elsewhere without first consulting him -- a promise I cheerfully gave. There followed two weeks of nerve-wracking silence. Then, another phone call -- would I come to his home in suburban Philadelphia on Sunday morning to discuss a position in his administration? Yes, indeed!

George Harkins, who had been my student intern during the 1970 campaign, drove me to the Governor-elect's home in Merion, just outside Philadelphia. Shapp and I left George to make conversation as best he could with Mrs. Shapp, and headed for a nearby deli. There Shapp (the first Jewish governor in the history of Pennsylvania) was mobbed by the predominantly Jewish clientele. It was at least a half-hour before we could get any time to ourselves. When we did Shapp wasted no time: would I become his legislative secretary, with full responsibility for shepherding his legislative program through the General Assembly?

Before giving him my enthusiastic "yes" I made two points. One was to remind him that I had supported Bob Casey in the

1970 gubernatorial primary. He laughed, and said simply, "We all make mistakes." The other issue was more serious. I wanted some major administrative responsibility to test the proposition that, although as a lawyer in solo practice and as a legislator I gained little administrative experience, I could nonetheless be a competent executive. I was particularly interested in serving as Secretary of Education. I come, on my father's side, from a family of teachers and preachers; someone once calculated that amongst them my father and his ten siblings had more than 150 years of teaching in the public schools. My father himself was a college administrator most of his adult life; my mother served a term as an elected school board member; my sister was trained as an elementary school teacher; and her husband, my former college roommate, was a professor of chemistry. In addition to all this, I have long believed that an outstanding public school system is good medicine for many of the defects of our society. So the Governor and I reached an understanding: I would serve as the Governor's legislative secretary, but if he ever decided to jettison David Kurtzmann, the Secretary of Education whom he had inherited from Governor Shafer, he would take seriously my desire to serve him in that capacity. Cynics might think this a poor deal from my standpoint – a promise on my part to serve him now in return for a vague promise to "consider" my qualifications to be Secretary of Education at some time in the future; but I had confidence – justified, as it turned out – that the Governor would be true to his word.

Shortly after the Merion meeting I was invited to accompany the Governor-elect and several of his closest aides on a "working vacation" at the Pinehurst Country Club in North Carolina. Apart from golf, which I didn't play, we were occupied with recruiting a staff and a cabinet. I don't recall that my advice was of any particular importance, but as I had no candidates for staff or cabinet to push I was in a position to offer some fairly objective judgments, a fact which may actually have increased the weight of what little advice I put forward.

Shapp was an anomaly in more than one way. The New York Times, assessing his strengths and weaknesses in 1976 as a presidential candidate in a generally favorable review, concluded that if he were not short, Jewish, unprepossessing in appearance and a poor public speaker, Milton Shapp would make an admirable candidate. But what distinguished him in my mind from most of the other senators and governors I have known were two qualities: his creativity and his compassion. Most politicians who succeed at the statewide level are not especially creative people, relying chiefly on staff for ideas. Their function, in addition to the symbolic one, is to act as a sieve, winnowing out the non-starters: the politically unattractive ideas and the policies that are superficially attractive but impractical from a budgetary or administrative point of view. With Governor Shapp it worked the other way around. He was a fountainhead of ideas, good, bad, and indifferent; the task of his staff was to select and refine the 10% of them that were truly admirable. The Governor's brain never rested; it was not unusual for Cabinet or staff to get a late-night phone call – "Can you come up to the Mansion -- I have an idea!" Happily, he could usually be persuaded to postpone the discussion to a more civilized hour.

Governor Shapp had been a pioneer in the cable TV business as well, where he was reputed to have made $13 million before he went into public life. At a cocktail party I professed some bewilderment, given his somewhat chaotic style of management, about how had he ever made that much money. His close friend and advisor, Dr. Zalmon Garfield, spoke up: "Pitt, you're asking the wrong question." "What's the right question?" "How come he didn't make $113 million?"

Shapp's compassion reached not only classes of people – especially the elderly and the poor – but individuals as well. Conservatives have sometimes accused liberals of caring more about justice in the abstract than about justice toward real people. That couldn't be said about Milton Shapp. One morning I came in early to discover him already at his desk, poring over a large Geodetic Survey map of Lancaster and Lebanon counties. He was upset by the fact that the State Fish Commission, in creating the new Middle Creek Wildfowl Refuge, was going to flood the house of a long-time resident of the area. The Governor, an engineer by training, had figured out that by moving a dam downstream the Commission could spare the house. He wanted me to go into court immediately, on his behalf, to seek an injunction against the Commission. It took the combined efforts of Dick Doran, his chief of staff in all but title, and myself to persuade him that the issue had been thoroughly litigated and that further efforts would be a waste of time. (The Governor didn't have much use for lawyers, and this incident probably confirmed him in that prejudice).

On another occasion, the Governor was perturbed to read in the local papers about a high school soccer player who had been suspended by his coach because of the length of his hair. (It's hard to believe, but at one point in American history that was a burning – or should I say, a cutting! – issue). The Governor's immediate instinct was to order the boy reinstated. In the end he acquiesced, with great reluctance, in my view that he had no such authority, but vented his irritation by issuing a press release deploring the school's judgment and saying that he was more interested in what was going on inside the boy's head than in what was on top of it, a judgment with which I heartily concurred.

As legislative secretary to the Governor, I was responsible for his entire legislative program. This involved not only pushing administration bills, but also figuring out where we stood on a host of other measures and promoting or derailing them as circumstances required. It was a mammoth job, and at first I had very little help, apart from Jackie White, my loyal and enthusiastic secretary.

Sometime in the spring of 1971 I was given permission to hire an assistant and, on Dick Doran's recommendation, took on Bill McLaughlin, a young and ebullient Irishman who had been teaching school in New Jersey but was knowledgeable about Pennsylvania politics. I found him to be trustworthy as well as diligent. And the legislators liked him personally, which really helped; I venture to think we made a good team.

My job was made much easier by virtue of the fact that Ernie Kline, the Lieutenant Governor, assumed most of the responsibility for shepherding Shapp's legislative program through the State Senate, where we had a tenuous 25-24 majority with one vacancy. Ernie had been a state senator and minority leader, and knew his colleagues and their foibles. He and Shapp were not well acquainted when they ran separately for Governor and Lieutenant Governor in the primary of 1970, but they teamed up easily afterwards and turned out to be, I think it's fair to say, the most effective gubernatorial pair in recent Pennsylvania history.

The Governor's office was, to put it mildly, disorganized. This was partly by design. Shapp didn't want a chief-of-staff; he said it prevented good ideas from reaching him. But Dick Doran, who had the only other office besides mine communicating directly with the Governor, was "primus inter pares" and someone I looked to for advice and assistance on a regular basis. He was first rate: bright, tough, and acerbic; without his leadership the whole operation would have fallen apart.

Shapp was both a good talker and a good listener; consequently, no appointment ended on time. A fifteen-minute meeting lasted a half hour; a one-hour meeting often stretched to two. It was not unusual, at 5 p.m., for the Governor to be still in the 3 p.m. meeting; Dick Doran would be soothing the 4 p.m. visitor while I made small talk with the 4:30 p.m. appointment and the 5 p.m. guest cooled his heels in the Reception Room. The only advantage of this "system" was that I got to spend time with some interesting people. I especially remember a half-hour with Senator John Heinz (also an Exeter graduate) who was recovering from a skiing accident; his death in an airplane crash some years later was a tragedy, not only for his family, but also for the people of Pennsylvania.

The key to influencing the Governor was, of course, access; you had to know what meetings were taking place, and to be able to insert yourself into the ones that concerned your area of responsibility. The staff was a bit casual about keeping people informed, more, I think, a matter of negligence than malice. I got in the habit, early on, of engaging Kit Boyd, the Governor's very loyal personal secretary, in ostensibly idle conversation while glancing over her shoulder at the Governor's calendar to make sure I wasn't being left out of some meeting that touched on my legislative duties.

It was thus that I discovered one day early in 1971 that the Governor planned to meet with Harry Boyer and Mike Johnson, President and Vice-President, respectively, of the state AFL-CIO. They had supported Shapp in both the primary and general elections of 1970. What, I asked Kit, was the meeting all about? She was evasive, but eventually confessed that it concerned amendments to the workers' compensation law. Didn't she think the legislative secretary ought to be present? Yes, she did, and so I was included.

Harry and Mike arrived in their usual truculent humor. After some pleasantries, they got down to business: labor wanted major amendments to the workers' compensation law expanding the list of those eligible, liberalizing benefits and streamlining procedures. As they described each one, the Governor gave his enthusiastic assent. I became increasingly apprehensive, both because of the cost of the amendments to the business community and the difficulties involved in getting them through the legislature. Two or three times I attempted to slow down the steamroller, to no effect. By the time the meeting ended, the Governor had endorsed all the amendments and put their implementation in my hands.

After Harry and Mike had left I screwed up my courage and said: "Governor, wouldn't it be more prudent to listen to their advice without comment, and then tell them that you would ask staff for an analysis of their suggestions and get back to them within a week or so?" The Governor gave me a look that suggested I had a lot to learn, and that ended the matter. I was naive in not realizing that labor's support in the campaign had given Harry and Mike something like a blank check which they were in the process of cashing. At any rate, we ran the amendments, got most of them through, and in the process lost considerable support in the business community.

Like most other politicians, Governor Shapp wanted to please people; the problem was that in pleasing them he sometimes damaged himself. We learned early on that we needed to have a reliable staff person in every meeting; if the staffer couldn't prevent the Governor from making unwise commitments, he could at least bear witness to the exact nature of those commitments.

Having never held public office, Shapp did not possess a well-developed sense of what was politically possible. That, plus his congenital optimism, sometimes resulted in his promising more than he could deliver. I remember Dick Doran giving me a draft of the governor's inaugural speech, containing some language to the effect that there was "no problem so difficult that we cannot solve it if we put our hearts and minds to it." I wrote in the margin, "No! No! No!" telling Doran that one of the reasons why politicians were held in poor esteem was their tendency to over-promise. Pat Moynihan has some useful things to say on this point in his essay, "Politics as the Art of the Impossible." But the offending language stayed in.

A good deal of my time as legislative secretary went into meetings with lobbyists; seeing me was often a sort of consolation prize for not being able to see the Governor. Their entreaties ranged from the sublime to the ridiculous, but it was necessary to display respect if not enthusiasm for these exercises of the ancient right to petition. On one such occasion I received a delegation of masseurs and masseuses from Allegheny County. They were much exercised by the tendency of the Pittsburgh press to treat massage parlors as though they were all fronts for houses of prostitution. In order to elevate the status of their profession they had hit upon the idea of creating a statewide licensing board dominated, naturally (there was ample precedent for this), by practitioners.

After hearing their case I explained as gently as I could that the governor had a low opinion, which I shared, of the many licensing boards which already existed and was unenthusiastic about adding to their numbers. At this point the chairman of the delegation pulled from his raincoat pocket a dog-eared copy of Stephen F. Bailey's little treatise, "A Bill Becomes a Law," and said, rather plaintively, "Mr. Pittenger, I've read this book three times and it don't have your name in here anywhere." Some years later, when Bailey and I were both teaching at Harvard, I recounted this episode, prompting him to say that he hadn't known he was taken so seriously.

In addition to my legislative duties, the Governor asked me to serve as liaison to the Department of Education. He had retained the Secretary from the previous Republican administration, Dr. David Kurtzmann, a short, gentle, thoughtful man, born in Czarist Russia, trained as an economist and active in the Pennsylvania Economy League. I'm sure Dr. Kurtzmann chafed at having to report to someone as callow as myself, but he was too polite (or too discreet) to let his feelings show.

In 1971, Kurtzmann played a major role in preventing Penn State from making a very serious mistake. The University had hired as president John Oswald, the former president of the University of Kentucky. Oswald succeeded Dr. Eric Walker, a Harvard-trained engineer noted for his political conservatism (he once boasted to a legislative committee of which I was a member that there were only a handful of card-carrying Communists on the campus, "and we have our eye on every one of them"). From my point of view, Oswald was a breath of fresh air, talking not only to students, a useful quality in the early '70s, but to the presidents of other colleges and universities in Pennsylvania, who had largely been ignored by Walker. But from the point of view of the Old Guard on the Penn

State Board of Trustees, those were negative qualities, not positive ones, and they plotted to get rid of him.

Sometime in 1971 Dr. Oswald went into the hospital for a heart condition. Kurtzmann, who as Secretary of Education was an ex-officio trustee of the University, found out that the chairman of the Board was planning on calling a special meeting, ostensibly to give Oswald a leave of absence (which he did not want), but in all likelihood to ease him out. Kurtzmann suggested he and I see the governor, and I readily agreed. We laid the matter before Shapp, who was properly outraged. He authorized Kurtzmann to call the Chairman of the Board, making it clear that the Governor would look askance on any attempt to remove Oswald or diminish his authority. The call was made and had its intended effect; nothing more was heard of the coup, and Dr. Oswald served the University with distinction for many more years.

The focus of my year as Governor Shapp's legislative secretary turned out to be our narrowly successful effort to pass the state's first personal income tax. It had become apparent during the 1970 gubernatorial campaign that the existing state tax structure would not yield a balanced budget, as required by the state constitution, for the fiscal year beginning July 1, 1971 without drastic budget cuts. The Republican candidate, Lieutenant Governor Raymond Broderick, had ruled out a personal income tax, a stand for which he was roundly criticized by some of the more responsible newspapers. Shapp was more cautious. He took the view that while he hoped he could balance the budget by running the state in a business-like

way, he would not rule out a personal income tax. By January, it was clear that we could not survive without it.

So the drafting and passage of such a tax became our top legislative priority, to which everything else was subordinated. The Governor would have preferred a graduated tax but settled in the beginning on a 5% tax based on federally taxable income. I was not directly involved in drafting the bill, but began lining up votes in the House, where we had a majority of 112-90. We made it clear to Democratic members that none of their pet bills, highways, or judicial appointments would go through unless they voted for the tax. Some members believed that a vote for the personal income tax was political suicide; one, a member of the Mushroom Club, burst into tears in my office as I made it clear that we expected his vote. Some tried to drive hard bargains; one demanded the Governor's support in a race against U.S. Senator Hugh Scott in 1972 (I told him to get lost). Shapp recruited members of the business community, many of whose leaders saw the fiscal wisdom of a personal income tax, to lobby Republican House members, with limited success.

The issue went down to the wire. On February 13, Fineman and Irvis kept the House in a rare Saturday session, but Irvis warned us privately about noon that several Allegheny County Democrats had booked flights home on a late afternoon plane and were determined to leave. We had to "roll the bill" by mid-afternoon. About 2 p.m. the last vote fell into place, and the bill passed the House 103-97, one vote more than the bare minimum needed under the Pennsylvania Constitution, which requires a majority of the total membership rather than a majority of those present and voting. One Republican supported the bill and ten Democrats defected. I was both elated and exhausted.

Attention then shifted to the Senate, where Ernie Kline went to work. We had a 25-24 majority, with one vacancy, but under the Pennsylvania Constitution we needed 26 votes, an absolute majority, so we had to have at least one Republican vote. We found it in the form of Senator Fritz Hobbs of Schuylkill County, who was from a wealthy coal-mining family and had been elected with strong labor support. But although we had Hobbs' support two Democratic senators, Nolan and Duffield, were now off the reservation. Senator Ben Donolow (D, Philadelphia) then proposed to amend the bill by lowering the income tax to 3.5% but raising business taxes to offset the loss of revenue, a bill which Nolan and Duffield could support. In that form the bill passed the Senate 26-22, was concurred in the House 106-90 and signed by the Governor, amidst quiet rejoicing by the staff, the following day. We had gotten most of what we needed to keep the Commonwealth solvent for the next several years, but the business community paid a heavy price for its inability to get any Republican senators other than Hobbs to support the income tax at 5%.

Our elation was short-lived. On June 21 the state Supreme Court handed down a 5-2 decision holding the income tax unconstitutional under the uniformity clause of the state Constitution. We knew from previous court decisions that the Court would strike down any attempt at a graduated tax, but our legal advisors thought that a flat tax, based on federal tax liability, could pass muster. We were wrong – victims, I suspect, of the Pennsylvania system of electing judges and the raw partisanship which that system breeds.

There was no alternative to rewriting the bill, re-submitting it and going through the whole exercise all over again. This we did through the hot and sticky summer of 1971. In order to placate the Supreme Court, the revised bill imposed a flat 2.5% tax (later reduced to 2.3%) on eight separate categories of income and raised certain business taxes. I will say for the Democrats in the House that for the most part those who had promised their support stuck by us. The passage of time helped by making it clearer each month that we could not balance the budget without an additional major source of revenue. This time 12 Republican House members and 6 Republican Senators supported the tax in return for increases in school subsidies largely benefiting Republican districts. We got the second bill through the House on August 25 and the Senate on August 31; Governor Shapp signed it into law on August 31. In my view the personal income tax was Shapp's greatest legislative triumph; it put the Pennsylvania state budget on a fiscally sound basis for several years and enabled us to avoid the traumas even now being experienced in states like New Hampshire and Tennessee which have lacked the courage to enact some form of state income tax.

There were at least two lessons to be learned from the passage of the income tax. The first was that no major tax initiative could be pursued successfully without the strong support of the governor. Although most Democrats and many Republicans conceded privately that passage of the tax was necessary, personal and partisan considerations often trumped the general welfare. It helped enormously that the state constitution had been amended in 1968 to allow the governor to serve two successive terms; unlike his predecessors, Shapp was not a lame duck as soon as he was reelected. Without the clout stemming from that fact we probably would not have succeeded. The other lesson was that if you wanted to effect major change, you couldn't be too scrupulous how you went about getting it. The Commonwealth will be paying for a long time for the roads, bridges, and dormitories that paved the way for votes in favor of the income tax, and about that I have no regrets.

It might seem odd that I herald the passage of the personal income tax as the principal achievement of the Shapp Administration. But the most important thing a government does is to raise and spend money. A governor may have all sorts of bright ideas about how to improve education, health care, or the environment, but if the revenue isn't there, they will remain just bright ideas. Oliver Wendell Holmes, Jr. is supposed to have said, "When I pay taxes, I buy civilization." (I would have said, "When I pay taxes, I buy the conditions that make civilization possible" – more accurate, but less eloquent.) The motto of the American Revolution was not, "No taxation," but "No taxation without representation." There is not much danger in a real democracy that people will be overtaxed; the danger lies in the other direction. It's not hard to find the votes for lowering taxes, but as I know first hand, it's a Herculean job finding the votes to raise or even to extend them.

The income tax was not our only legislative achievement. We merged a number of state agencies into a new Department of Environmental Protection, although the sportsmen, a powerful and tenacious lobby, fought successfully to maintain the Fish and Game Commissions as separate agencies. The state assumed responsibility for Lincoln University, a small predominantly black college in Chester County, founded by Quakers before the Civil War to educate free blacks. Act 101 established and funded an affirmative action program in the public colleges and universities. We also passed a constitutional amendment extending the vote to 18-year olds; made major changes in the school subsidy system; provided reimbursement to the parents of children attending non-public schools (later declared unconstitutional by the United States Supreme Court in *Meek v. Pittenger*); enacted a billboard control act and one to regulate strip-mining; and made major changes in the laws relating to unemployment compensation, eminent domain and escheat, among other things.

We also passed a state lottery bill. Although it was not part of the administration's legislative program, Governor Shapp was an enthusiastic supporter, chiefly because the net profits from the lottery were earmarked for programs benefiting senior citizens, whom he regarded in many ways as his most important constituency. I spoke against the bill in staff meetings, arguing that while it was true that a certain amount of gambling would inevitably occur, it was profoundly immoral for the state government to lure citizens to their own destruction. I lost the argument, but not my conviction.

An increasing amount of academic research suggests that state-sponsored lotteries, casinos, and other forms of gambling have greatly increased the number of Americans who gamble regularly, often with serious damage to themselves and their families. Nevertheless the lottery is now such an integral part of our revenue system, contributing $680 million per year to the state budget, that it would be politically impossible to repeal; in fact, the 2003-4 session of the legislature passed and Governor Rendell signed a bill to allow slot machines at racetracks and other venues, the proceeds aimed in part at helping reduce the burden of school property taxes.

My year in the Governor's office did nothing to improve my view of the Fourth Estate. Television coverage was often ludicrously simple-minded, and even the major newspapers got things wrong. The Pittsburgh Press once printed a story about a proposed gas tax increase which contained a number of factual errors. I pointed them out in a letter to the Press which they declined to print. A story in the Harrisburg Patriot criticized the governor's staff for insulating him from public opinion. Given the lengths to which he went to crowd every possible petitioner into his schedule, that seemed far-fetched; in fact, the instigator of the story was not a member of the general public but a staffer who thought he was not getting Shapp's ear as often as he should, and took revenge by "leaking" the story about Shapp's "isolation."

A more serious charge against the media is that they punish failure more energetically than they reward success. The Shapp administration was a genuinely innovative one -- I would argue the last such in Pennsylvania. We tried many things. Some worked, some did not, but the "gotcha" style of journalism which has come to prevail made us pay a heavy price for the failures. My unhappy conclusion is that a newly elected governor has two choices: he can pursue an ambitious agenda, knowing that there will be failures as well as successes and that he will be punished for the failures far more severely than he will be praised for the successes, or he can play it safe -- balance the budget, deal with emergencies and take no chances. If I were consulted by a governor-elect facing this choice, I would (against all my natural instincts) urge the path of caution, and indeed, that seems to be the strategy that the Thornburg, Casey, and Ridge administrations have pursued. Ed Rendell's victory in 2002 represents a return to a more ambitious agenda, but the fact that he faces a hostile legislature makes me dubious about the outcome.

By the time we sent the General Assembly home in October of 1971 I was exhausted. I had shepherded not one but two income tax bills through in addition to keeping track of a raft of other measures. I had alienated some of my Democratic friends, especially in the House, with the strong-arm tactics we had employed in getting the tax bills passed. And I was becoming somewhat disenchanted with the management style of the Shapp administration -- the chaos in scheduling, the failure to put any one person in charge, and the tendency to bite off more than we could chew. It was time to pursue the pledge I had extracted from Shapp when he asked me to be his legislative secretary -- that he would take seriously my interest in serving as Secretary of Education, a post newly created by the Constitutional Convention of 1968.

Chapter 8 - Top Bureaucrat – Staffing and Organization

The Governor announced my nomination to be Secretary of Education at a press conference in December of 1971. Unfortunately, in answer to a question from one of the reporters, Shapp said he had given me a quiverful of darts and instructed me to throw them at every door in the department; wherever the dart stuck I was to fire everyone inside. It took me at least a year to overcome the suspicions aroused in the bureaucracy by that single casual remark.

My nomination was not an especially popular one. The press was skeptical, and some education groups were downright hostile. Republican senators blocked the nomination, which required a two-thirds vote and thus some Republican support. Senator Wilmot Fleming, the ranking Republican on the Senate Education Committee, assured me privately that the Republican caucus was holding up my confirmation not out of animosity toward me, but as part of their continuing jousting with a Democratic governor. So I was "acting secretary" for almost a year until finally, on November 30, 1972, the Senate relented and confirmed my nomination by a vote of 47-0.

My public position was that so long as I had the authority and the salary, I couldn't care less; privately, I was irritated by what appeared to be a gratuitous insult. Some of the opposition related to my ties to Franklin and Marshall College, which were alleged to pose a "conflict of interest." As Secretary of Education I had one of twenty votes on the Board of the Pennsylvania Higher Education Assistance Agency, which made policy for state scholarship and loan programs. The argument was that because I was an untenured adjunct professor at Franklin and Marshall College, I was bound to favor the private over the public colleges in devising eligibility standards for both programs. That argument seemed far-fetched and never carried much weight with the legislature or the press.

More than once I was asked how someone who had never taught in a public school could make good policy for public education in Pennsylvania. One such query came from an elementary school teacher in a Temple University summer school class taught by Pauline Leet, my future wife. After pondering the question for several seconds, I said by way of reply: "Here are five problems sitting on my desk at the present time:

1. Should I fight the Attorney General over his action in bringing a sex discrimination suit against the Pennsylvania Interscholastic Athletic Association when I think the State Board of Education could better resolve the issues?

2. Should we introduce an administration bill in the House or Senate, and with what sponsors?

3. Do I have the legal authority and the political will to undo what in my judgment was an unwise consolidation of four school districts in Mifflin County?

4. How can I get rid of an unsatisfactory employee who is civil service and protected by his immediate supervisor?

5. Should I waive the requirement of a letter of eligibility for the new Superintendent of Schools in Philadelphia?"

I then asked my questioner how my having been a classroom teacher would have helped me to answer any of these questions. She conceded that it would not -- but that did not stifle the critics. Only my performance in office could do that.

The terms on which I became Secretary showed that I had learned a few things since my first plunge into politics. I understood that my bargaining power with the Governor was at its zenith on the day before I said "yes" and declined rapidly thereafter. Serving as liaison between Governor Shapp and Dr. Kurtzmann had opened my eyes to some of the conditions necessary to succeed as Secretary of Education. I insisted upon, and got the Governor's agreement to, three conditions:

1. There would be no one (i.e., no John Pittenger) on the Governor's staff acting as liaison to the Department of Education; I would have direct access to the Governor as often as needed.

2. I would select my own staff and deputies; the Governor could veto any of my choices, but he could not foist off someone who was unacceptable to me.

3. As far as educational boards and commissions were concerned, I would name the members of the State Board of Education, subject to the Governor's veto. With boards of trustees of the public colleges and universities, it worked the

other way around: the Governor could name them, subject to my veto.

Governor Shapp was scrupulous in observing these ground rules. We quarreled only over two or three state college trustee appointments where Harvey Thiemann, the Democratic state chairman, was pushing candidates whom I considered unsuitable, and over a state college presidency where I thought the candidate being promoted by Democratic politicos was too young and lacked vision. On the latter issue the Governor called me in and said, "Pitt, if I have to choose between you and the Majority Leader of the Senate, you know who I will favor." I nodded reluctantly and withdrew my opposition.

The department I took over in January of 1972 was a sprawling bureaucracy, its 1,100 employees occupying most of a five-story neo-classical building a stone's throw from the Capitol. We shared the building with the State Library, administratively a part of my domain, and a very small Department of Banking. The chief architectural feature of the building was the Forum -- an ornate semi-circular auditorium seating 2,000 with a star-studded ceiling and uncomfortable seats. It was (and is) home to the Harrisburg Symphony and many civic events.

Until 1968 the Superintendent of Public Instruction, as he was then called, served a fixed four-year term, beginning and ending in the middle of the governor's term of office, on the theory that education policy ought to be insulated from politics. Amendments recommended by the Constitutional Convention of 1968 and approved by the voters changed the title to Secretary of Education and made its occupant serve, like the rest of the Cabinet, at the pleasure of the governor. So my years in office were a test of a new system as well as a new Secretary.

I was acutely aware of the fact that under the new dispensation the Governor could fire me on a minute's notice. In talking with students about careers in politics I have always emphasized the importance of financial independence. It was a source of comfort to me to know that if the Governor ever asked me to do something really distasteful, I could always practice law or retreat to the farm and grow enough food to keep body and soul together. Fortunately, in the six years I worked for him, Governor Shapp never asked me to act in a way that would have offended my conscience.

All but 10 of the 1,100 departmental employees were civil service. It was a system run on the usual lines -- written examinations, bonus points for veterans and the "rule of 3" in filling vacancies, i.e., I could only select from among the persons with the three highest adjusted scores. The predictable result was a department staffed mostly by white males with roots in the public school system. To some extent the department functioned as a "half-way house" for school superintendents worn out from battling school boards and teachers unions but not quite ready for retirement. They were not, taken as a whole, a very creative lot. But there were many outstanding individuals who only needed a bit of encouragement to blossom.

Luckily I inherited a superb trio of secretaries in my own office. Barbara Geist was a gem; she wound up serving nine secretaries with loyalty and discretion. On more than one occasion she rescued me from the consequences of my own folly. Two younger but equally devoted people, Chris Gallo and Nanette Kimmel, handled the phones and the mail. The three of them made a formidable team.

David Hornbeck, who eventually became Executive Deputy, was a Texan who earned graduate degrees in theology and law at Union Theological Seminary and the University of Pennsylvania, respectively. While in law school he served as Chairman of the Board of the Philadelphia chapter of the Americans for Democratic Action, and was thus acquainted with everyone in Philadelphia's liberal political community. David was set to clerk for Judge Abraham Freedman at the Third Circuit Court of Appeals when Freedman died suddenly of a heart attack. Israel Packel, Governor Shapp's Attorney General, invited David to join his staff in Harrisburg, which he did in August of 1971. During the next several months David and I worked together on several issues of interest both to the Governor and the Attorney General, and came to respect one another; so it was natural, when the Governor asked me to take over the Department of Education, for me to invite him to come with me as Special Assistant and Counsel.

Soon thereafter we began a search for an Executive Deputy Secretary, the No. 2 position in the Department. We unearthed some first-rate candidates but all eventually turned us down. I then received from David a memorandum, handwritten, on lined legal-size yellow paper, outlining all the reasons why I should make him the Executive Deputy. So well reasoned was the memo that I acceded to his request – and never regretted doing so. I came to refer to this document as David's treatise. It was the first of several, all equally persuasive.

I mention this incident, not only to suggest one of Hornbeck's outstanding qualities, but to illustrate a different point, namely, the need for people in government to be able to express themselves clearly, forcefully and persuasively in writing. Much of the prose in government documents is insufferably pompous, muddled, boring or all three. So to come across a written statement that summarizes the facts accurately, lays out the options crisply and evaluates them sensitively is doubly rewarding. So majoring in English is not so impractical after all – assuming, perhaps without warrant, that all English majors have developed the capacity to write good prose.

David and I were a good team -- the Blanchard and Davis of the Pennsylvania Department of Education. I was "Mr. Outside," dealing with the press, the Governor, the General Assembly, and the myriad organizations making up the educational universe. David was "Mr. Inside," putting budgets together, fighting with the Civil Service Commission over job descriptions and with the local unions over conditions of work, and, most importantly, helping set goals and priorities for the next several years.

I had generally good relations with the press, largely, I think, because I didn't try to conceal anything from them. But they were seldom able to ask questions that would have elicited meaningful answers. One young reporter from a daily in central Pennsylvania was so inept that I finally said, "Look, let's make a deal; I'll interview myself, and you write down the answers." We proceeded along those lines. Two weeks later I got an ecstatic call; he had been promoted on the basis of the article he had written on his interview of me! Would I be his guest at dinner? Yes!

In my five years as Secretary of Education I was seldom surprised by any question put to me at a press conference or in a legislative hearing. I attribute that fact to having surrounded myself with able and candid people who would alert me at the first sign of trouble. But I wasn't immune to the desire to hear only the good news. One hot Friday summer afternoon Hornbeck popped in with some unwelcome news, namely, that we would have to ask the General Assembly for a supplemental appropriation for Vocational Education. It had been a bad day, and I exploded – "Dammit, David, why don't you give me some good news for a change?" He shrugged his shoulders and left. Monday morning David came in beaming. What was so amusing, I asked? "The pigeons have quit shitting on the window sills." "Why the hell are you telling me that?" "You wanted some good news, and that's the only thing I could think of."

My relations with the legislature were generally cordial as well, and for the same reason – candor – combined with the fact that members of the House had, I think, a certain pride in the fact that one of their own had been promoted to a Cabinet position. And it helped that I did not voice the usual educational clichés.

At a Senate Appropriations Committee hearing I was challenged by Senator Richard Snyder, a very conservative state senator from Lancaster County (and a partner in Barley, Snyder, Cooper and

Mueller, my former employers): "Mr. Secretary, you have spoken several times about the value of a liberal arts education. Could you describe these values to us?" I thought a minute, and remembered a story of my father's about his senior year at Indiana University. He was taking a philosophy course, and on the last day of the semester the professor went around the class asking each student what he proposed to do after graduation. One would go into banking, another work in his father's factory, another to medical school. Finally, he came to a soft-spoken lad from Kentucky who, as the professor knew, had attended college at great financial sacrifice to himself and his family. The young man replied: "Well, sir, I am going back to Hardin County to farm tobacco like my pappy and my grandpappy." Professor: "In that case, why did you come all the way up here to Bloomington to study philosophy?" "Well, sir, I just wanted something to think about while I was following the plow." Senator Snyder made no reply. Moral: a soft answer turneth away wrath.

On the other hand, I learned early on that I could not depend on some members of the bureaucracy when it came to testifying before legislative committees. I recall vividly a hearing on Title 1 of The Elementary and Secondary Education Act in which a member of the House put an especially obtuse question to one of my staff, who began his reply by saying, "Representative, if you had been listening to my earlier testimony..." I cut him off quickly to prevent further damage.

Because I was not well known around the state and some of the Administration's policies were controversial, I spent several days each month visiting schools and colleges. It was not uncommon for me to take off from the airport in the Governor's plane at 7 a.m., land in some distant county at 8:30 a.m., meet separately with students and teachers, lunch with administrators, visit classes, end up dining with school board members, getting back to Harrisburg at 10 p.m., exhausted, but nonetheless stimulated.

For the most part I enjoyed these excursions as a welcome change of pace from the bureaucratic life. They also served as a platform from which to puncture misconceptions about the state's role in public education. Often, in the question and answer session which followed a talk to school board members, someone would ask why Department regulations prevented them from doing something they wanted to do. "But they don't," was often my reply. "But our solicitor says they do." "Well, your solicitor is wrong." (Having been trained as a lawyer helped at this point.) Sometimes I got the impression that school board members would prefer to blame things on Harrisburg rather than to accept responsibility for the quality of education in their districts.

The issue that confronted me most often on these field trips, and one that continued to exacerbate relations between the Department and the school districts, was that of "unfunded mandates." The demand that each state mandate be accompanied by appropriations sufficient to defray the cost of implementing it seems plausible on the surface, but there is a practical difficulty: such a regime would create an administrative nightmare for both the state and the districts. In fact there were pressures to do the opposite, i.e., to reduce the number of separate funding streams in order to give school districts more flexibility. But the critics have a point: there is a strong tendency on the part of legislatures to impose burdens without paying for them. After all, if you can have the pleasure of being able to say to your constituents that you have "solved" some problem while escaping the pain of having to foot the bill, you are living in what is politically the best of all possible worlds.

So the right question, as I kept telling my critics (to no great effect), was not whether the state was imposing a particular mandate while making school districts pay for it, but whether the overall level of state support for public education justified the cumulative burden of all the mandates issuing from the legislature and the State Board of Education. Thirty years ago, when the state was supplying about 55% of total instructional cost, my answer to that question tended to be "yes;" today, the state's share having declined to about 35%, it would be much easier to say "no."

On a field trip to Greene County, in the far southwest corner of the state, I was asked by a school board member whether I thought a superintendent ought to be required to have a doctorate in education. I said, "no," and added: "In fact, I think every doctorate ought to have a notation at the bottom of the diploma – P.S., the conferral of this degree does not imply omniscience." Afterwards, a grizzled school board member came up to me and said, "Mr. Secretary, I'm a Republican; I've been a school board member for 32 years; and that's the most sensible thing I've ever heard from a Secretary of Education."

But sometimes in the field I got myself in trouble. In an English class in Red Lion, York County, I asked if they had ever read H.L. Mencken's story, "The Girl from Red Lion, Pa." No, they had not. So I told them about the girl who took a tumble in the hay with her boyfriend on a Saturday night. Waking, convinced she was a fallen woman, she took the milk train to Baltimore, where she asked the hack driver to take her to the nearest house of ill repute. The madam, horrified by the notion of this lass becoming a professional, fed her a good breakfast and put her on the next train back to York. It is a charming story, but it got me an indignant letter from the president of the Red Lion school board demanding to know why I was subverting the morals of the younger generation.

On one of the field trips I acquiesced in a request by a Democratic state senator to hitch a ride back to Harrisburg on the Governor's plane. We ran into some dirty weather and soon the pilot was ducking in and out of thunderclouds. The senator was looking a bit pale so I enquired how he felt. "I'm OK," was the reply, "but I can't go down now – too many fuckin' scores to settle."

Hornbeck's mild exterior and East Texas twang concealed an iron will, which was both his greatest strength and, occasionally, a liability. It enabled him to carry through projects which would have daunted a less committed person, but it blinded him to the fact that not everyone is a true believer. Some of his plans could have succeeded only if implemented by people with his brains and zeal. Alas, there were not many such people to be found. But I have said publicly more than once that though politically somewhat insensitive he is the ablest person I have worked with in public life, and I haven't changed my mind about that. He went on to be Superintendent of Public Instruction in Maryland for twelve years, a chief architect of Kentucky's much-praised school reforms, and Superintendent of Schools in Philadelphia and President of the International Youth Foundation.

Too many legislative and administrative initiatives are based on unrealistic assumptions about the people and resources necessary to carry them out. A classic case of a mismatch between means and ends is the "Leave No Child Behind" Act, the centerpiece of the Bush Administration education policy. The intention is admirable; the likely outcome, less so. IF school districts could decipher what they are supposed to be doing under the terms of a mammoth and complex statute; IF children could be persuaded to take seriously the battery of examinations required by the Act; IF school districts didn't cut corners in an attempt to inflate test scores; IF there was an adequate supply of qualified teachers willing to teach in urban and remote rural schools; IF there were vacancies in neighboring schools to which children in failing schools could be transferred; IF the prospect of losing students to neighboring public and private schools didn't demoralize rather than energize the staff of the failing school; and (most important of all) IF the resources were available to do all that is required to be done, then the Act would be a resounding success. But each one of these conditions that cannot be satisfied, especially those relating to resources, reduces the chances of attaining the goals of the Act. It is simply not a piece of legislation that bears much relationship to the real world.

People often say of a public policy, "it was right in theory but wrong in practice," but there's something odd about that statement. Theory should take into account the probable conditions under which a policy will be carried out – the probable level of funding, the likely prejudices of the people in charge, and the level of public support. If the Act in question can only succeed under optimal conditions, doesn't that suggest a faulty theory?

In addition to David and my personal secretaries I was permitted to hire one special assistant, someone not protected by civil service, who could help me in a wide variety of ways. For two years that post was filled by Deb Weiner, an education activist from Philadelphia recommended to me by Hornbeck. Deb wielded a wicked pen – her description of graduate schools of education as "cesspools" in a speech written for me did nothing to endear me to that fraternity – but she was good at cutting through bureaucratic red tape. She also drafted a memo to the staff outlining my expectations about the prose quality of documents submitted to the secretary; Ernie Doerschuk, the state librarian, later told me with some amusement that it had caused a small stampede of staff coming to the library to look up the meaning of "passive voice." When Deb left to become an assistant dean at Temple Law School her place was taken by Dick Deasy, a former Christian brother and newspaper reporter, who managed to get things done without raising quite so many hackles.

Apart from my personal staff the only positions in the Department not covered by civil service were the two commissioners -- Basic Education and Higher Education -- and their deputies. From Dr. Kurtzmann I inherited in the former position Dr. B. Anton Hess, a long-time superintendent, well respected by his colleagues both in the department and in the field. But after working with him for two months I concluded that he and I were not on the same wavelength, and asked for his resignation, which was forthcoming. He was soon hired as Executive Director of the Pennsylvania Association of School Superintendents, a position from which he harried my right flank for the next five years.

With the Governor's approval I promoted Don Carroll to Commissioner. Don, a former superintendent, had been with the Department for several years. He had the respect of his colleagues; he also had drive and imagination, qualities he quickly displayed in getting us some Rockefeller money to fund the first Governor's School for the Arts in the summer of 1972. As Don's deputy we installed Harry Gerlach of Lancaster County, a staunch Republican; my hope was that his appointment would assuage the feelings of those who had been wounded by Dr. Hess's departure, and in this I think we were largely successful.

Higher Education was less politically charged, which made the search for a Commissioner a bit easier. Eventually we settled on Jerome Zeigler who had been involved in creating an alternative campus at Purchase in the State University of New York. He was a delightful colleague and soon earned the respect of the college and university presidents with whom he worked closely.

We used a variety of strategies to try to inject some life into a rather inert bureaucracy. One was to persuade the Civil Service Commission to define job qualifications more flexibly. Many positions required, for example, an earned doctorate and so many years of administrative experience, which made it difficult to find qualified women and minorities, groups which had for many years been excluded from the qualifying experiences. We urged the Commission, with some success, to add "or equivalent experience" to the existing requirements, or to loosen them in other ways.

Another strategy was to take seriously the annual civil service evaluations, which asked the supervisor to rank the employee's performance on a number of categories – promptness; ability to work with others; performance of assigned tasks; creativity, etc. – as "excellent," "good," "fair," etc. Many employees had become accustomed to receiving "excellent" marks across the board. When David and I insisted that the evaluations be more realistic, there was much wailing and gnashing of teeth. I remain undecided to this day as to whether the gains justified the pains.

As part of our strategy to loosen things up in the Department, we organized a departmental softball league in the summer of 1972. The Governor called me one day asking if I could find a summer spot for the son of a good friend. I asked, "Can he hit and throw?" The answer was "yes" – he was Ed Zubrow, catcher for the Haverford College Varsity Baseball team. With Ed's help the Secretary's Office won the championship over Data Processing in a close contest, and then, to cap our summer, beat the Governor's Office captained by Dick Doran.

The central problem with running a big bureaucracy is that you can easily fill up each day just by reacting to the demands of other people – the Governor, the legislature, the public employee unions in the Department, the professional associations representing teachers, superintendents and principals, and many others. To make any real progress you need to seize the initiative and write your own agenda. For that purpose Hornbeck persuaded me to hold a staff retreat outside Harrisburg for the top fifteen or so Department officials, where we hammered out our priorities. Later David worked out systems for measuring progress toward these goals. I can't say it worked across the board, but it certainly helped focus our efforts more effectively than if we had simply continued to roll with the punch.

The Governor gave me as Secretary a great deal of autonomy, in legislative as well as in administrative matters. I don't think I abused my discretion, but sometimes I skated on thin ice. For example, the teachers unions were pushing for legislation that would have given control of teacher certification, then in the hands of the Department, to an independent commission dominated by teachers. I told them, without ever discussing it with the Governor, that if their bill passed in that form, he would veto it. By threatening a veto I succeeded in getting the bill watered down to a point where the new Commission would be merely advisory to the State Board. Fortunately for me, no one called my bluff.

The opposite sort of problem arose when the Governor was keen about some initiative that struck me as politically or administratively infeasible. One of his favorites was the notion of putting an office of the federal employment service in every high school in the state, as an antidote to teenage unemployment. In this case I had the good fortune to encounter at some Democratic function the United States Secretary of Labor, Willard Wirtz, whose department controlled the Employment Service. He quickly threw acid on the Governor's plan, saying that the Service was a hidebound bureaucracy which could not collaborate with public schools in any useful way. The Governor had enough respect for Wirtz to accept this advice as dispositive.

Another Shapp project was what became known as the "Educational Trust Fund." The core idea was that expenditures for higher education ought to be regarded as an investment, not a current expense. In the Governor's view, college students should be able to borrow the full cost of their undergraduate education, paying off the loan over a lifetime at rates that would vary according to the graduate's income. On the surface the idea was attractive: it would have enabled people to attend college for whom the available loan and scholarship package was inadequate, and encouraged students to go into careers like social work, teaching and the ministry by allowing them to pay off their loans more slowly than their classmates who were striking it rich on Wall Street. I hope it was not just bureaucratic inertia that prompted me to pursue the Educational Trust Fund idea with less than total vigor. I could not persuade myself that such an ambitious undertaking could be implemented successfully at the state level; given the mobility of the American people, it almost had to be a national program, albeit one well worth further study. A number of states, including Pennsylvania, have since implemented plans to help families finance their children's collegiate education; none, as far as I know, vary the rate of payback according to the income of the student.

I spent a good deal of time during my first year as Secretary dealing with something called the "Business Review of State Government" which the Governor had established by executive order the previous year. It involved a number of highly placed business executives lent by their corporations, organized into task forces, and charged with finding ways to save state tax dollars. Shapp had two motives in organizing the review. One was to find out whether, in fact, the state could save money by adopting more business-like practices. The other was to buy some good will in the business community by soliciting their advice.

The task force assigned to the Department of Education made a number of recommendations. Some – the electronic transfer of subsidies from the state to local district, for example – made good sense. But some were marred by a lack of understanding of the political forces at work. For example, they wanted us to merge two state universities, West Chester and Cheyney, which were only 10 miles apart and which duplicated many academic programs. From a purely efficiency standpoint the recommendation made sense. But it did not take into account the fact that Cheyney, 95% black, was viewed by the African American community in Philadelphia as its university. Many African American lawyers, doctors, preachers, and business persons in Philadelphia had graduated from Cheyney and were intensely interested in its future. A proposal to merge it with West Chester, a much larger and predominantly white institution, would have aroused the most passionate opposition.

Another instance of the wide gap between politicians and business people was revealed when the Governor asked me to speak at a Saturday morning seminar to a group called The Young Presidents, business leaders who had made more than $1 million before they were 40 (Governor Shapp was a charter member). I gave a routine talk on the responsibilities of my department. In the question period that followed one of the CEOs asked, in a somewhat belligerent tone of voice, "why don't you run your department the way I run my corporation?" I wavered for five seconds between saying, "That's a stupid question" and enumerating some of the differences between a public and a private institution. Governor Shapp broke in to say, "Pitt, would you mind if I tackled that question?" I was only too happy to have him intervene – and the following dialogue (as best I can remember it, 30 years later) took place:

Shapp: How many members are on your Board of Directors?

Businessman: Fifteen.

Shapp: Who put them there?

Businessman: I did.

Shapp: Do you ever have divided votes?

Businessman: Never!

Shapp: How would you like to run an enterprise with a budget of $10 billion; with two boards of directors, one of fifty members, the other of 203; and with 24 out of the 50 and 94 of the 203 out to embarrass you in every possible way?"

Businessman: I never thought of it that way.

Putting business people in high political office is not a guarantee of success. The range of skills required by a governor goes far beyond the managerial skills which most successful business executives have cultivated including, for example, the ability to deal with the press on a daily basis. We continue to hear the demand that government be run in a business-like way, although recent revelations about greed and dishonesty on the part of top executives in some corporations and accounting firms may have undermined enthusiasm for this "solution."

The degree of autonomy entrusted to me by Governor Shapp was apparently not accorded to some of my successors. One of them called me in some bewilderment – had Shapp allowed me to telephone members of Congress without approval of the front office? Of course, was my reply. My caller then confided that he had just received an edict, applicable to all cabinet members, forbidding them to communicate with members of Congress unless they cleared it with the Governor's staff. I told him that I would have resigned. But this is the fruit of a strategy which would rather play it safe; ours, by contrast, was a risk-taking administration.

Chapter 9 - Top Bureaucrat – Policies and Politics

Although we were able to carve out time and resources for some of our own initiatives, to a considerable extent the Department's agenda was dictated by forces outside the Shapp Administration – the legislature, the Congress and state and federal courts.

Much of my time and energy during my first two years in the Department was taken up with the lawsuit which had been filed against the Shapp Administration in 1971 by the Pennsylvania Association for Retarded Children (PARC). The suit asserted that retarded children, many of whom were either in state institutions or at home but in neither case receiving any real instruction, were being denied a public education in violation of both the due process and equal protection clauses of the U.S. Constitution. Our attorneys concluded that the plaintiffs were essentially right, and so we negotiated a consent decree which the Governor signed in 1972. The decree committed us to locating every retarded child in Pennsylvania, assessing the child's needs, and providing an "appropriate education." Some school administrators were angry with me for not contesting the case more vigorously, but they were wrong, legally, morally and politically. The PARC decree is often cited by courts as legal authority for the right to a free public education for all handicapped children and was one of the principal sources of the 1975 federal act, the Education of All Handicapped Children Act (EAHCA); it also won general favor with the public.

The Governor's School for the Arts was one of our most successful initiatives. It began in the summer of 1972 with about 150 students from all over the state, selected on a competitive basis and housed for five weeks on the campus of Bucknell University. Several features were unique. The faculty were not public school teachers but distinguished professionals: a jazz musician from Pittsburgh, the retired first violinist of the Philadelphia Orchestra, a choreographer with the Pennsylvania Ballet, etc. Each student selected a major and a minor. All were committed to going back and strengthening arts programs in their respective schools. At the end of the five weeks they put on a program showcasing their achievements. The first summer Governor Shapp and I attended their program. He played the violin and I sang Gilbert and Sullivan, both of us off key.

In addition to honing the talents of individual students the Governor's School for the Arts had a number of beneficial side effects. Many of the intermediate units were inspired to create day programs to accommodate students who were not quite good enough to make the final cut for the residential program. In some districts the students who had taken part lobbied their school boards against cuts in arts programs. And the Thornburg Administration subsequently created Governor's Schools in mathematics and the sciences, health care, education, and international affairs. I can't vouch for their quality, but I applaud the effort to involve more young people in the practical application of academic skills.

Many of the things we wanted to do required the support of the State Board of Education, which had been created in its present form in the 1950s as a way of subjecting some areas of educational policy to review by a well-informed and essentially independent body. In some states the Board is elected, and thus has its own power base; in a few the board actually appoints the chief state school officer. But in Pennsylvania the Board consisted of 17 members appointed by the Governor and confirmed by the Senate for overlapping six-year terms. It had played a major but politically controversial role in the sixties, carrying out legislation to reduce the number of school districts in Pennsylvania from 2000 to 504. Much of its time was devoted to reviewing state and federal regulations.

Students of educational policy-making at the state level have generally concluded that state boards are the creatures of the state secretaries of education, no matter what the formal relationship. That was not quite the case in Pennsylvania. When I went to Governor Shapp in 1972 with my first list of recommended board appointments, his question was, "Do you want a weak board or a strong board?" I said, without hesitation, "A strong board," and meant it. I wanted a Board that might occasionally disagree with me, but that could be genuinely helpful in selling our policies to the education world and the general public.

For my purposes a bipartisan Board was crucial. Thus we reappointed Republican James Rowland, an African American attorney from Harrisburg, and appointed other Republicans such as John O. Hershey, Principal of the Milton Hershey School, and Don Fox, a former Republican member of the House. Among our Democrat appointments were Don Rappaport, of the Philadelphia office of Price Waterhouse, and Keith Doms, Director of the Free Library of Philadelphia. Madge Benovitz, an independent from the Wilkes-Barre area, was a former state-wide president of the League of Women Voters. I regret that Governors Thornburg and Ridge chose to abandon the bi-partisan approach; by 2002 there was not a single Democrat among the seventeen gubernatorial appointees. What the Governor may have gained in creating a compliant board has been overshadowed, in my judgment, by having a board with less credibility. I am glad to see that Governor Rendell has returned to the practice of making bipartisan appointments.

My relationship with the State Board was sorely tested on several issues. Early in my tenure I had decided to create a student advisory board -- not just because I wanted to get some sense of what young people were thinking, but because I enjoyed their company and felt isolated from schools and colleges in Harrisburg. So I created by executive order a Student Advisory Board consisting of one student from each of the 29 Intermediate Units, chosen by the students themselves. The Board decided to tackle the drafting of a "Statement of Student Rights and Responsibilities" (this was the early 1970s when many young people were alienated from the "establishment" by the war in Vietnam). My political antennae were not working very well; I would have been better advised to put more emphasis on the "responsibilities" and less on the "rights." But we plowed ahead, holding hearings around the state, and eventually putting before the State Board a proposed statement in September of 1975.

All hell broke loose. The document itself was not very radical, for the most part simply codifying existing federal and state law. In some areas it was even conservative; for example, I resisted the pleas of some of my staff who wanted to abolish corporal punishment, leaving that still in the discretion of local school districts. But the prevailing opinion in the field was of a radical document, and local educators, especially school boards, bitterly resented the notion that the state had any legitimate role to play in regulating student conduct.

The State Board adopted the Statement of Student Rights and Responsibilities with only minor changes. But that did not end the controversy. The Girard School District in Erie County filed suit against me and the Board, asserting that we had acted without legal authority, and persuaded a number of other districts to join the suit and contribute to its costs. The Commonwealth Court, a specialized court hearing mostly cases involving state government, agreed with Girard, and by a vote of 5-2 overturned the Board's regulation. But in 1977, after I had left state government, the Pennsylvania Supreme Court unanimously reversed the Commonwealth Court, saying, in effect, that where K-12 was concerned the Board and the Secretary could adopt any policies not clearly prohibited by the state constitution or statutes. Thus the plaintiffs not only failed to overturn our regulation, but opened the door for more sweeping assertions of state authority in the future. Moral: leave well enough alone.

A second issue that got me and the Board in political hot water involved women and sports. Control of interscholastic athletics in Pennsylvania rested, in the first instance anyway, not with the Board or the Department, but with something called the Pennsylvania Interscholastic Athletic Association (PIAA), a private body dominated by high school principals and athletic directors. It tended, in any clash between academic and athletic values, to prefer the latter. PIAA's Rule 22, stipulating that girls could not practice with, or compete against, boys had been invoked in the case of a female cross-country runner who worked out with the boys' team because she left the other girls far behind. We thought this was pretty stupid and debated how to deal with the issue.

I would have preferred to go the regulatory rather than the litigation route, on the grounds that the State Board was in a position to craft a more nuanced policy than the courts. But the Attorney General thought otherwise, and insisted on bringing suit against the PIAA and its Rule 22. We eventually won on that front when the Commonwealth Court, in an opinion by Genevieve Blatt, its only female member, held Rule 22 to be unconstitutional under the state constitution. In the meantime the Board and I proceeded with a much more detailed regulation requiring equal treatment of women in interscholastic and intramural athletics: equal coaching, facilities, and schedules, among other things. It evoked a good deal of hostility – there was much snide talk about women wrestlers, and the Lieutenant Governor warned me at one point that my policies would lose Shapp the forthcoming election in western Pennsylvania, a hotbed of male chauvinism. But we persevered, and in the Fall of 1975 the Board adopted the final policy, which became a model for Title IX, the principal federal legislation in this area. Its implementation went much more smoothly than anticipated, and today, when I drive past fields of girls playing soccer or softball, I am pleased to think that we played even a minor role in opening these doors.

My satisfaction at having promoted wider girls' participation in high school athletics was balanced by my chagrin over an unintended but not unforeseen side effect, namely, the professionalization of women's athletics. I had anticipated this development in a talk I once gave to a group of women involved in athletics and recreation, entitled, "Before You Ask For A Piece of the Pie, Make Sure There are No Maggots In It." I warned the women that in seeking equal treatment they were running the risk of buying into all the evils associated with men's programs. The results were as predicted. A recent study of college and university athletics, "The Game of Life," by William Bowen and James Shulman, documents the trends: as women's athletics have become "big time," the academic achievements of female athletes relative to men have steadily declined. Women intercollegiate athletes used to have better high school records, to perform better academically in college, and to have more impressive post-collegiate careers than their male counterparts. No longer: women athletes now display most of the academic weaknesses of their male peers.

The Board and I did not always agree, but we hashed out our differences privately. Jane Freedman, a Board member from Philadelphia, was keen to extend to gifted and talented students the due process rights which had been granted to handicapped children under the PARC decision. I opposed such a move on the grounds that it would unleash a flood of lawsuits by the parents of every budding musician or astro-physicist seeking special treatment for their children through the courts. The Board sided with Mrs. Freedman and adopted the regulation; so far as I can tell it has had neither the dire consequences which I predicted nor the beneficial results sought by the Board.

Two other departmental ventures had less happy outcomes, in part, at least, because of my still-limited political understanding of the forces at work. Don Carroll persuaded me that we should appoint a "Citizens Advisory Commission" to study the whole K-12 system of public education in Pennsylvania, and to make recommendations for change. We instructed members of the Commission not to pay any attention to the political feasibility of their recommendations, and they didn't. So they presented us with a large and fascinating report filled with suggestions for change -- but the report was politically DOA. In retrospect, we should either have given the commission a more modest frame of reference or, if we really wanted to upset the applecart, we should have focused more carefully on preparing the way for its acceptance.

A similar fate befell our attempts to modernize the Pennsylvania School Code, which had last been systematically updated in 1949, and was full of anachronisms. On this point there was general agreement. But agreement went no further; as soon as the task force, ably chaired by Mark Widoff, started proposing specific changes, consensus broke down. None of the major players -- school boards, superintendents, principals, or teachers -- wanted to make concessions without knowing what concessions would be required of them in turn. And that, of course, we couldn't say. The School Board Association, which I had already offended in a variety of ways, refused to believe that I did not have a secret agenda beyond improving the workability of the whole system.

Much of the opposition stemmed from fear of the unknown. For example, the Pennsylvania Supreme Court had ruled consistently that school districts had only the legal authority specifically granted them under state law. This resulted in a massively complex school code, since every time a court held some activity to lie beyond the scope of current law there was immediate, and often successful, demand for a legislative amendment. We therefore proposed to reverse the basic assumption: that is, to incorporate into the school code the premise that school boards had any power not prohibited to them by the state constitution or statutes. I naively thought that such a clause would be popular with the School Board Association. Not so! They preferred to live in a world where they could blame their failures on a lack of authority from the state instead of one in which they would have to accept full responsibility, power not being at issue.

In retrospect I now understand that I had a choice between two basic administrative models in my dealings with schools and colleges. One was what I will call the consensual model: let the various interest groups (teachers, school boards, administrators and parents) fight it out, mediate where that seemed called for, and ratify the result. This was essentially the model that had been followed by my predecessor, Dr. Kurtzmann. The advantage of such an approach was less wear and tear on the Secretary and the Department and less political risk to the Governor. Against that we had to weigh the fact that the interests of children and of the general public were sometimes overlooked. The other model, which I will call participatory, is one where the secretary becomes a player seeking, at least on some issues, to influence the outcome from the beginning. As a member of the Shapp Administration there was never much doubt which side I would come down on – advocacy was our middle name – but I wish in retrospect I had been clearer in my own mind about the political risks of such an approach, or more skillful in dealing with them as they arose.

As Secretary of Education I automatically became a member of the Council of Chief State School Officers, an association of state and territorial education leaders which existed mostly to lobby the Congress and the President. Because of my political background I quickly became a member, and then chairman, of the Chiefs' legislative committee, orchestrating, with the help of some very able staff, such activities as the successful attempt to override Nixon's veto of the Health, Education, and Welfare budget in 1975 and a less successful attempt to obtain more funds with which to implement the EAHCA.

I started out advocating a vigorous federal role in education, but my experiences over the next five years tempered my enthusiasm. The central problem was not only that Congress was unwilling to appropriate adequate funds in support of its various initiatives, but also that the conditions attached to the receipt of money were often grossly disproportionate to the amount of money involved. Even the present Supreme Court majority, which in other areas of the law such as the scope of the interstate commerce clause has been willing to police the boundary between national and state power, has failed us here; in answer to state complaints that they are being coerced by the conditions attached to federal money, the Court has a simple answer: don't take the money! But this is politically unrealistic, a fact which Congress understands much better than the Court. No governor, for example, would dare to reject federal money to implement the Education of All Handicapped Children Act, although federal dollars have never exceeded 15% of the total cost of the program as against the 40% promised in the legislation. (There are signs that some states are beginning to rebel against the imbalance between obligations and resources in implementing the "No Child Left Behind" Act; I wish them well).

Nor were members of Congress and their staffs shy about throwing their weight around. I found myself one day in the office of Representative John Brademas (Democrat, Indiana), then chairman of a subcommittee of the House Committee on Education and Labor. My mission, on behalf of the chiefs, was to obtain a greater degree of flexibility in the administration of the EAHCA. I ended up talking to a twenty-something lawyer on Brademas' staff. "Mr. Secretary," he finally said, "you don't seem to understand; we regard you as part of the problem, not part of the solution." That seemed to me to be a curious view since Congress was placing on the states the primary responsibility for carrying out the mandates of the Act. But it was a view that prevailed on the Hill, even among avowedly more conservative members.

Some years later, when I was a law school professor, I had a chance to promote federalism in a very different context, as a member of the Advisory Board to the State and Local Law Center. The Center had been established to help state and local governments in putting their best foot forward in cases before the Supreme Court, since that is a highly specialized form of legal advocacy. We were occasionally rewarded by a footnote citing a brief which our very small paid staff, or our pro bono attorneys, had assisted in preparing, but I'm doubtful that we did much to stem the inexorable flow of power to Washington, a development presided over with equanimity by Republican as well as Democratic presidents.

I have come, reluctantly, to the conclusion that there are few principled defenders of federalism in Washington. Even members of Congress who were formerly governors or state legislators quickly forget what it is like to be on the receiving end of federal mandates. Conservatives rail against social and economic regulation, but tolerate federal interference in people's private lives; liberals deplore the latter, but encourage national control of economic and social policy. Even the political scientists have largely abandoned the cause of what is often described, along with separation of powers and a Bill of Rights, as one of the three outstanding American contributions to the theory of government.

One incident occurring during my stint as chairman of the Chiefs' legislative committee illustrates the value of a liberal arts education. In the spring of 1974 President Nixon was threatening for fiscal reasons to veto the budget passed by Congress for the Department of Health Education and Welfare. The education lobby, including the Chiefs, decided to mount a major effort to override the veto, and for that purpose scheduled a breakfast meeting, attended by several hundred state and local officials, the Monday of the week during which the vote was to be taken.

The principal speaker at the breakfast meeting was the flamboyant Dan Flood, a Democratic Congressman from the anthracite coal region of Pennsylvania and chairman of the HEW Subcommittee on Appropriations. As the education chief in Flood's home state I was invited to introduce him. Lying awake in my motel room the night before I tried desperately to think of something to say beyond the conventional platitudes. About 3 a.m. I had an inspiration. Flood had been a Shakespearean actor in his younger days and was fond of quoting The Bard. I remembered the scene in Henry IV, Part I involving Hotspur and Owen Glendower, the bombastic Welshman:

"Glendower: I can call spirits from the vasty deep."

"Hotspur: Why, so can I, or so can any man; But will they come when you do call for them?"

In introducing Flood the next morning I described him as a man who excelled at "calling spirits from the vasty deep" and noted that "when he calls them, they do come." (I misquoted Shakespeare, saying "summon" rather than "call," but no one seemed to notice).

Flood was elated, twirled his handlebar moustache and treated my department generously for the next year or two. And we won the override vote.

So far I have written principally about policy and politics affecting elementary and secondary education. But Pennsylvania is one of a handful of states in which the department of education has jurisdiction over all education, from pre-school through the PhD. Unfortunately, my exertions in the area of higher education were less strenuous than those in K-12 and not very productive. In part, that was the result of uncertainty about the authority of the Secretary and the Board over public colleges and universities. But it was also because colleges and universities are, in my experience, very nearly impervious to change, especially change coming from the state capitol.

Penn State dominated higher education politics in Pennsylvania; it had enough support in the legislature, solidified by the generous distribution of football tickets and other goodies, to do just about anything it wanted to do except in the matter of appropriations. In the regime of Dr. Eric Walker Penn State had made energetic efforts to locate a branch campus in every populous county in the state. It didn't quite succeed, but it came close enough to thwart the development of a really good system of community colleges, a severe blow to the state's hopes for economic development which has not been remedied thirty years later.

Although as Secretary I was an ex-officio member of the Boards of all four state-related universities – Penn State, Pitt, Temple, and

Lincoln – I made only ceremonial appearances at the latter three and concentrated my fire on Penn State, which had long operated as the academic wing of the Republican Party in Pennsylvania. Most of my efforts were the equivalent of a mosquito attacking an elephant. I voted against expansion of the football stadium; argued for awarding scholarships only on the basis of financial need; pressed the president to appoint more women and minorities to high administrative positions; and generally made a nuisance of myself. Believing that size is the enemy of quality, I pressed Jack Oswald, who had succeeded Walker, to hold enrollment on the main campus to 30,000: it is now above 40,000. And although it has some first rate departments, such as geography and some of the engineering schools, it isn't in the same league with the best public universities such as University of California–Berkeley and Michigan.

While a trustee of Penn State I became embroiled, through no fault of my own, in a tenure battle where I found myself on the conservative side, defending existing institutions and processes against an ill-informed attack by students. Wells Keddie was a popular but controversial professor of labor relations who had been recommended for tenure by his department but rejected by the Dean of Liberal Arts and President Oswald. When my state car arrived at the Nittany Lion Inn for a weekend trustee meeting I noted a crowd of students in front of the Inn chanting "We Want Pittenger. We Want Pittenger." My pleasure in this display of support curdled as it became apparent from their shouts and gestures that they were in a mood for a lynching, not a coronation. Instructing my driver to pull around behind the Inn before I could be discovered, I sent a message to the students: I would meet with some of their leaders for breakfast the next day, but I would not address a mob. Mollified for the moment, they dispersed. At breakfast the next morning they made their agenda clear: I was to override President Oswald and grant tenure to Professor Keddie. By way of reply, I told them that I had no legal authority to do what they wanted me to do, but that I would not rest my case on that basis alone.

I put to them a hypothetical case: Suppose the governor were not Milton Shapp, whom they generally admired, but Frank Rizzo, then riding high wide and handsome as Mayor of Philadelphia and a likely challenger to the Governor in 1974? And suppose the Secretary of Education was not John Pittenger but Max Rafferty, a right-wing ideologue who was my opposite number in California? And suppose Penn State had recommended tenure for Keddie? Would they be happy to have established a precedent by which Governor Rizzo, acting on the recommendation of Secretary Rafferty, would overturn the University's grant of tenure? The honest answer was – they didn't give a damn; they wanted justice in this case, and to hell with the long-range results. So late in the day, having rejected any further parley, I discovered on my walk to the gym three dummies dangling from the low-lying branch of a tree near the statue of the Nittany Lion: they were labeled "Oswald," "Paulson" (the Dean of Liberal Arts), and "Pittenger" respectively. I am, as a result, more skeptical about young wisdom than I used to be.

One of my tasks as Secretary of Education involved issuing teaching certificates to candidates who satisfied the relevant standards, which among other things required that a person be "of good moral character." The most difficult of those decisions involved a young man, a senior at Penn State, who surfaced as an officer of an undergraduate club devoted to furthering the interests of homosexuals.

The facts were that the applicant, who had done his practice teaching in the local school system, earned praise from his supervisors, his students and their parents; there was no evidence that his sexual orientation had in any way affected his teaching. To resolve the question of whether he was, under the circumstances, a person of "good moral character," President Oswald appointed a committee of six deans; to no one's great surprise deaconal wisdom split 3-3 throwing the matter squarely into my lap. The Attorney General, Shane Creamer, and I scheduled a meeting with Governor Shapp to discuss the legal and educational dimensions of the issue. The Governor first asked Shane what the law required; he replied, issuance of the certificate. He then turned to me and asked what sound educational policy suggested; I replied that since the young man had been an exemplary teacher and had violated no laws, we should issue a certificate. After a cursory discussion of the likely political ramifications of the decision the Governor simply said, "Boys, go and do the right thing."

With some trepidation I issued my decision to award the certificate at 4:30 p.m. on a Friday afternoon, when I figured the press room would be deserted, and flew that night to London for a well-earned vacation. My instructions to Barbara Geist were to leave me alone for a week, and then call me the following Friday. When she called, I asked what the fall-out had been from my decision. Her reply was: four letters in favor, four letters against, a nasty editorial in a small weekly in the boondocks and a plaintive call from the chairman of the House Education Committee asking, "Did Pitt have to make the decision this way?," to which she promptly replied, "yes," and that ended the matter. All this happened before Anita Bryant got started on her homophobic campaign; five years later we would not have gotten off so lightly. And I was deeply grateful to be working for a Governor who just said, "Go, and do the right thing."

My relations with the 14 state colleges, which metamorphosed from normal schools to colleges and (later) to universities, were far more intimate. Under the law as it existed in 1972 they were essentially run out of the Department of Education through something called the Board of State College and University Directors, with the Commissioner of Higher Education as the Board's executive arm. Each college had its local board, but these had become advisory only.

The Presidents were the focal point of my interest. It would be hard to say which gave me more grief, hiring them or firing them. Under state law the governor had the final say in their appointment. When a vacancy occurred the college would set up a search committee along the usual lines and let the process work itself out until the committee had given us three names. Inevitably local legislators got involved – to take care of their friends, to protect patronage sources, or simply as a matter of prestige. And the candidates they were pushing were not always well qualified. I remember one name that kept popping up every time there was a vacancy. He had no administrative experience, but that didn't prevent his sponsors from asserting that he would be "one hell of a president." We managed to hold him off during my term in office. And we managed to throw our weight onto the scales in favor of several candidates who had not come up the traditional ladder, but promised to bring a wider perspective to the job.

If hiring good presidents was a headache, firing bad ones was a nightmare. I fired three in five years, which is still a record. One was a basically decent person who had let things get out of control; the college was being run (in important respects) by the wrestling coach, who could do no wrong in the eyes of the local Board and the alumni. I sent Art Sinkler, the former CEO of the Hamilton Watch Co., to mediate; he recommended removing the President, the coach, and one other officer. I followed his recommendations. The president landed on his feet as Vice President of a much larger university; what happened to the other two I do not know.

The other two firings were equally painful. One involved a man with a military background who was under the impression that you could run a college pretty much the way you run a wing of the Air Force. He quickly ran afoul of the faculty union, and their battles kept the campus in a continuing turmoil. I remember addressing a rather hostile assembly of faculty and students, accompanied by

Stanley, my 10-year old nephew from Colorado. One of the faculty protesters carried a large sign, "Pittenger is a Boo-Boo," which made it onto the front page of the local papers the next day. Stanley reported to his mother that life in Pennsylvania was pretty exciting.

In the end I called in the President and asked for his resignation. He behaved very well, asking only that for family reasons he be given a one-term leave of absence with pay to tide him over the transition. State law made no provision for such an arrangement although it would have been routine in a private university, but we drafted a termination agreement that paid him as a consultant which served the same purpose. I took a copy to Bob Casey, Sr., then the Auditor General, telling him exactly what had happened, and asking that he not come down too hard on me. I'm happy to note that his subsequent audit of the transaction was critical but perfunctory.

My third presidential firing involved a president for whom football was top priority. He wanted to install a press box at the football stadium. When the Department vetoed his original plan he attempted to evade that disapproval by letting a series of contracts for amounts that were below the threshold requiring Departmental approval. He also waived out-of-state tuition for several football players from Ohio, which we thought he lacked the authority to do. I wound up going to the campus and addressing a largely hostile audience about our reasons for thinking he should be removed. That was a mistake. He ended up suing me and the Department; settling the suit eventually cost the Commonwealth a bundle.

I saw very little of the 70,000 or so students then enrolled in the state college system, with two exceptions. One involved an internship program, which I organized in 1973, with the college faculties selecting 15-20 students to spend a semester in Harrisburg. We found them jobs in agencies suited to their interests: for example, a math major might be assigned to the computer section of PHEAA, or a music major to the Pennsylvania Council on the Arts. The interns were responsible for finding their own living quarters. One evening a week we met in my spacious apartment overlooking the Susquehanna River for a seminar on state government. Our guests included the Lieutenant Governor, legislators, newspaper reporters, lobbyists, legislative staff, and civil servants. The program worked, at least from my perspective, extraordinarily well. One unanticipated benefit was some friendships which have lasted to this day.

My other point of contact with students resulted from the Governor's desire to have a student appointed to the board of trustees of each of the fourteen state colleges. There was no legal impediment to our doing so – the Governor had unfettered discretion in appointing the nine-member boards, subject to confirmation by the Senate – but the political cross-currents were tricky. In the end we worked out a process by which the campus forwarded three student names to the Department; I interviewed them and recommended one to the Governor. We neglected to specify that the student trustees would serve only so long as they continued to be students; at least one student trustee took the position that his appointment was good until the end of the six-year term (he now sits in the House of Representatives). I also helped the students in the system organize a state-wide body to lobby Harrisburg more effectively; in the long haul that was probably a more significant step than appointing student trustees.

My relations with the state college faculties were strongly colored by the fact that the General Assembly had in 1969, with my support, passed a statute allowing public employees, including state college faculty, to organize, bargain, and strike. The first bargaining sessions with the faculty union, the Association of Pennsylvania State College and University Faculty (APSCUF), began in 1971. By statutory design the state's interest in faculty salaries and benefits was protected by being bargained between the faculty union and the Governor's Office of Administration; on non-salary issues the Department of Education spoke for the state. The first round of bargaining by the Office of Administration resulted in salaries which were out of line with those in other institutions, for which I took quite a bit of heat from my friends in private higher education. But the Department wasn't much better, being guilty (I now think) of centralizing too much authority in the state and leaving too little discretion to the individual campuses. Subsequent contracts partially redressed the imbalance, but I continue to regret our failure to create a more "federal" system, i.e. one in which policies are adjusted to meet local circumstances.

On one occasion the Department made common cause with the faculty union in curious circumstances. In 1974 President Nixon imposed a wage freeze, which Washington interpreted as disallowing part of the faculty salary increase we had granted in the most recent round of negotiations with the faculty. Dave Hornbeck and Marty Morand, the Executive Director of the faculty union, came up with an imaginative solution: take the money thus blocked and use it to create a series of distinguished teaching and research awards, which were deemed not covered by the wage freeze. For two years this worked well: then the faculty soured on it, canned Morand, and we reverted to a more adversarial stance.

*   *   *

By the spring of 1976 I was running out of steam. Hornbeck, with my blessing, had departed to become Superintendent of Schools for the State of Maryland. Don Carroll had left in 1975, to be replaced by Frank Manchester, a forward-looking superintendent from the Lower Merion School District. Deb Weiner had taken a position as Assistant Dean at Temple University Law School, only to discover that she had traded a job with a modest title and lots of clout for a job with a good title and very little influence. Mark Widoff, sadder but wiser after our failure to obtain passage of the revised School Code, became Consumer Advocate for the state, a position created by the Shapp Administration in which he served with great distinction. And I myself was exhausted by the struggles over education of the handicapped, Student Rights and Responsibilities, women's sports, the funding of the state colleges, and many other only slightly less compelling issues.

Moreover, my relations with the Governor were less cordial than they had once been. I attributed this partly to the influence of his wife, Muriel, a bright and energetic woman who took Eleanor Roosevelt rather than Bess Truman as her model. She championed the cause of a Yugoslav doctor who claimed to have made a major breakthrough in the treatment of deaf children, setting up a clinic in the basement of the Governor's mansion, greatly to the displeasure of the departmental experts in this area. She also sought to interfere from time to time in teacher certification decisions and didn't like being told by me that I had no legal authority to do most of the things she wanted me to do. (It didn't help that I once described the Shapp's son, Dick, an aspiring singer, as the "Margaret Truman" of the Shapp Administration). Her conclusion was that I had been "captured by the bureaucrats" – a conclusion I'm sure she shared with the Governor.

The other source of friction was my fault entirely. It was clear after his reelection victory in 1974 that Shapp, feeling less challenged by the job of being Governor, was looking for new fields to conquer. His successful intervention with the independent truckers during the 1973 gas shortage had given him a national profile and encouraged him to think ahead to the presidential election of 1976, when Gerald Ford would be running and defending his pardon of Richard Nixon. I was not enthusiastic about Shapp's presidential ambitions, judging them to be unrealistic. In addition, I worried that they were undermining his ability to govern the state. There were already signs, as in the criminal prosecution of one of his Cabinet members, that the administration was beginning to unravel.

The Cabinet was summoned to the Executive Mansion sometime early in 1976 by Zalmon Garfield, the governor's closest friend and advisor, and given its marching orders for the campaign. I chafed, and was only restrained by the greater wisdom of Carl Dellmuth, Secretary of Banking and an old family friend, from making a fool of myself. Unfortunately things did not end there. A reporter asked for my off-the-record opinion about the Governor's candidacy, and with more wit than wisdom I said that in my judgment he was trading a 50/50 chance of being the best governor of this century for a 1 in 1000 chance of becoming president. A front-page story in the Philadelphia Inquirer quoted an "unnamed Cabinet officer" to this effect.

Unfortunately I had used those very words in a private conversation with Dick Doran the previous day, so he had no trouble identifying the culprit. I received a phone call from the Governor: would I come see him immediately? I would, and did. Had I uttered the offending sentiments? I had, and justified them as best I could. He probably should have fired me on the spot, but he was much too nice a man to do that; he simply nodded his head sadly and said that he thought I underestimated his chances, considering that he had fooled the pundits more than once in the past.

As I look back on this episode it strikes me as a classic case of the sort of compartmentalizing of issues that was part of my intellectual baggage. It was of course true that when Shapp offered me the position of Secretary of Education it didn't involve an explicit pledge of support for his further ambitions. But that is beside the point. He had plucked me out of relative obscurity and made me, first, his legislative secretary, and then one of his top Cabinet officers. He had backed me up 99% of the time. I owed him in return more loyalty than I displayed. I now think there were only two honorable courses open to me: to resign immediately, if I felt that strongly about it, or to swallow my doubts and soldier on. I did neither, and to some extent forfeited his confidence as a result.

Thus things lay when in the spring of 1976 I received a phone call from Paul Ylvisaker, Dean of the Harvard Graduate School of Education (HGSE), asking if I was ready to come and teach at his institution for two years. The invitation was not totally unexpected. Paul had taught briefly at Swarthmore, where my parents knew him, and had been hospitable to me in London during my sojourn at the London School of Economics. In the Fall of 1974 I had, at his invitation, spent two weeks at HGSE, giving guest lectures and meeting with graduate students. It didn't take me long to say "yes" to the Dean's invitation. When he asked what kind of a salary I would require, I stupidly said $15,000; I suspect he would have paid me twice that amount. At first I was called a Visiting Professor. When members of his faculty complained that I was a mere practitioner, and thus not entitled to the honorific "professor," I became a Visiting Lecturer.

When I gave Governor Shapp my resignation he extracted a promise that I would not leave until my successor had been identified and at least nominated, if not confirmed. That promise cost me a term at Harvard. Paul had wanted me to begin teaching in

September of 1976, but it took the Governor until December to settle on Carol Kline, a professor at the University of Pittsburgh, active in Democratic circles and sister of Senator Wayne Morse of Oregon, as my successor. So it was not until early in January 1977 that I loaded up a pick-up truck and headed for Cambridge.

Looking back on those five tempestuous years as Secretary of Education, I wish I had known at the beginning what I had learned by the end. But it has been the nature of my life to have been thrust into (or sought) positions for which I was in significant ways unprepared. I don't think the public welfare has suffered as a result, but that is a judgment for others to make.

Chapter 10 - Sabbatical

In many ways my 18 months at the Harvard Graduate School of Education (HGSE) were a tonic, a wonderful way to decompress after five years on the griddle. Dan Steiner, a friend and law school classmate, then Legal Counsel to President Bok, found me ideal living quarters: a suite in Adams House belonging to the Senior Tutor, bound for England on a sabbatical. It was spacious, well furnished, a short walk from Harvard Square and HGSE and, best of all, about fifty feet from the intramural squash courts.

I taught three courses at HGSE: the Politics of Public Education, with Jerome Murphy, later the Dean; Law and Education with Walter McCann, later head of the American School in Athens; and, solo, The State Role in Public Education. My courses attracted a small but eclectic group of students, the majority of them from HGSE, but a few from the law school and the Kennedy School. The course with Jerry Murphy was a special pleasure: the two of us would meet for an hour before each class, plotting our respective roles. Usually Jerry was cast as the naïve academician (which he certainly was not), and I as the jaded practitioner. Sometimes, to the confusion of the class, we switched roles. I don't, on the whole, have a very high opinion of co-teaching, which too often takes the form of two quite separate courses jammed together, but ours was a genuine collaboration.

My writing took two forms. One was a report to the people of Pennsylvania on my stewardship of the Pennsylvania Department of Education, bearing the pedestrian title of "Progress and Problems in Education." Re-reading it 25 years later I am struck, on the one hand, by the relative honesty of my account; and, on the other, by my continuing naiveté as exemplified by my failure to anticipate the brouhaha over the School Code revision. Obviously I was a slow learner.

The other writing was an essay "Elliptical Billiard Balls" (a phrase borrowed from Gilbert and Sullivan's <u>Mikado</u>) outlining my views about the proper relationship between Washington and the states in making educational policy. My thesis was that while the national government was good at redistributing money, as for example, under Title I of the Elementary and Secondary Education Act, it was much less successful at bringing about changes in behavior, such as those required by the Education of all Handicapped Children Act. The student-edited Harvard Educational Review, to which I submitted the essay, rejected it on the grounds that it constituted an apology for Reagan's educational policies, which was nonsense. I never got around to submitting the article to anyone else, although parts of it eventually found their way into an article which Peter Kuriloff of the University of Pennsylvania faculty and I published in 1982 in the Public Interest, a neo-conservative journal.

I was greatly surprised one day in the Spring of 1977 to receive a phone call from the office of Governor Michael Dukakis: would I come over to the State House and give him some advice about public higher education? The Governor, a Swarthmore College graduate, was two years behind me at Harvard Law School, where I had known him at best casually. We spent a very pleasant hour together, although I was hard pressed to give him any really useful counsel. Public higher education has been a step-child in most of the Northeastern states, the public universities having been founded long after private institutions were firmly established; they are seldom adequately funded by the states.

My work with the Governor had a curious aftermath. I was describing our conversation some days later to a small group of people, only to have one them explode: "By God, the son-of-a-bitch has time to talk to someone from Pennsylvania, but he hasn't got time to listen to a state senator from his own party." The person making this statement was, as it turns out, the state senator in question; and the episode illustrated the continuing clash between the older, largely Irish Catholic wing of the Democratic party and the younger more progressive reform faction, a division which plagues the party in Massachusetts even today and has resulted in the election of several Republican governors.

Apart from teaching and writing, I played squash, organizing an Adams House team, which to everyone's surprise won the intramural title two years in a row. I also went to many of the concerts, plays, and lectures, which as an undergraduate I had neither the time nor the funds to indulge in. And of course much socializing – dinners with old Harvard friends and visits to Henry Bragdon, my prep school history teacher and mentor, in Exeter.

What I did not do was plan for the future. I'm sure that when Paul Ylvisaker invited me to Harvard, he intended it not only as a sabbatical from politics but as a vantage point from which to plan my next moves. But I was having too much fun to pay attention to the future, with consequences which will shortly unfold. So I returned to Pennsylvania in June of 1978 with no job and no immediate prospect of one. I did have one task – chairing a commission on the reform of the Pennsylvania House of Representatives – which I undertook partly to keep busy and partly to keep my name in the lights.

The Harrisburg press gets worked up periodically about the sins of the legislature. Usually these are venial rather than cardinal, but they cannot be ignored. The previous year the Philadelphia Inquirer had published a series of articles alleging the usual abuses. Leroy Irvis, by then Speaker of the House, concluded these charges should not be ignored; with Republican support, he decided to appoint a commission to study the situation and make recommendations for improving the internal organization and procedures of the House. He asked me to chair the Commission, and after ascertaining that its other members were people with whom I could work, I readily agreed.

The composition of the commission and my own prejudices guaranteed that its recommendations would be practical rather than radical: we had no intention of presenting a report that could not be endorsed and carried out by the House. Among my colleagues on the Commission were George Bloom, former chairman of the Public Utility Commission and fund-raiser par excellence for the Republican Party, and my good friend, Sidney Wise, of the Franklin and Marshall College faculty, author of a treatise on the Pennsylvania legislature. For staff we hired, on Irvis' recommendation, a young graduate student from the University of Pittsburgh. Apart from refusing, on feminist grounds, to fetch our lunches, she worked out reasonably well. We met almost weekly from July until October. At the first meeting, we adopted certain ground rules: among others, all decisions would be unanimous, and we would avoid the thorny subject of legislative compensation.

My first – and only – crisis as chairman occurred at our first meeting. One colleague, a faculty member at the University of Pittsburgh, wanted to know what provision I had made for obtaining a verbatim transcript of our proceedings since, in his judgment, these might be of value to future scholars. I had made no such provision, nor did I wish to make any, since in my view we needed to be able to discuss matters with a candor that was unlikely to prevail if our proceedings were being recorded. But how to say this to the professor without offending him? I was pondering this delicate question when George Bloom (whom I had thought asleep) raised a finger. "Mr. Chairman," he said, "I am a very old man, and sometimes I say very foolish things. I wonder if the Professor would extend me the courtesy of not putting my foolish thoughts on the record." Presto – my problem was solved; chalk another one up for the professional politicians!

Our report, published in October of 1978, made a number of recommendations, none of them earth shaking, but cumulatively important. Chief among them was to separate housekeeping from political responsibilities, and to have the former supervised by a Bi-Partisan Management Committee. This recommendation was put into effect the following year, along with many others, either by House Rule or by legislation; the House operates today essentially along the lines we laid down in 1978. Our success, such as it was, lay in the fact that we accepted the limitations of our assignment and sought only incremental improvements in the way the House disposed of its business. That didn't satisfy the press, which would have preferred something more radical if politically impossible; I continued to think that a bird in the hand is worth two in the bush.

Chapter 11 - Politics Ain't Beanbag

Our report filed, the question naturally occurred, what next?

I thought I knew the answer: the United States Senate!

Senator Richard Schweiker had announced in 1977 that he would not seek re-election in 1980. Looking back 25 years it is hard to imagine that I could have deluded myself into thinking that I was a plausible senatorial candidate. But I did: and for no better reason than thinking I would make a good senator. I still think that, but I also know that my qualifications were largely irrelevant in determining the outcome.

One sometimes hears it said of a politician that he is "too ambitious," but that seems wide of the mark. You don't become a governor or a Senator, let alone President, without being ambitious. My problem was that my ambition extended to the ends but not the means; while I would have liked to be a Senator, I couldn't bring myself to pursue it with the necessary intensity. Yeats says in one of his poems that a man must choose between "perfection of the life and of the work." But I did not want to make that choice; I wanted to attain high office without sacrificing my enjoyment of books, music, friends, and the other things that make life worth living. But it can't be done, at least by anyone with my modest talents and resources.

It should have been a signal to me that some of my closest friends, like John Hartman and Sidney Wise, were notably unenthusiastic about my Senate campaign. They were too polite to say "don't," although if I had been any good at reading body language I would have gotten the message. But I plowed blindly ahead.

The choice of a campaign manager proved troublesome. For a long time I deluded myself into thinking I could enlist the services of Sam Katz, an aspiring young politico from Philadelphia. While still an undergraduate at Johns Hopkins he had come to the attention of Herb Fineman who gave him a summer job with the House Democratic caucus. As I was then still Research Director for the caucus, and supervising the summer interns was one of my responsibilities, I came to know Sam well and to have a high opinion of his political acumen.

Sam and I stayed in touch over the next ten years. Eventually he became CEO of Public Financial Management, a firm that advised municipal governments about bond issues and debt management. He spent a good deal of time in late 1978 and early 1979 giving me advice. I assumed, without asking him point blank, that he would be willing to play a major role in my campaign. When he ultimately said "no" I was disappointed, viewing him as having led me down the garden path. I'm sure Sam has a different perspective. He later switched parties and narrowly missed being elected Mayor of Philadelphia in 1999, losing to John Street by only 9,000 votes; in a rematch in 2003, Street beat him by 80,000 votes.

In the end, I hired a young Georgian named Chip Smith who had some campaign experience at the Congressional level, but had never run a statewide campaign. He was further handicapped by not knowing much about Pennsylvania politics. The advice he gave me, however, was mostly sound, and I absolve him from any responsibility for the ensuing debacle.

Part of the problem lay in my inability to articulate a theme – a reason why people should vote for me. In a reversion to my earlier mind-set I had concluded that a reputation as an honest, bright, and hard-working legislator and cabinet member would be enough. It wasn't.

As further evidence of my naiveté I tried to persuade Chip that we ought to make the proper relationship between federal and state power a central theme of the campaign; it was something I felt strongly about and it seldom got addressed in campaigns, for what I now understand are good reasons. Chip persuaded me, correctly, that federalism had no gut appeal to the voters of Pennsylvania (or any other state). There is, moreover, something paradoxical about running for an office on the premise that you will not use the full powers of the office being sought. It was a classic case of my predilections getting in the way of clear thinking about the choices in front of me.

Other themes might have been more appealing. One with special relevance to Pennsylvania would have been the plight of the working poor, i.e., people who have full-time jobs but don't earn enough to support a family at even a minimally comfortable level. Tax policy would have been central to such a campaign, including advocacy of what became known as the earned income tax credit, but many other areas of public policy would have been equally important. David Riemer, a former student of mine at Harvard and for many years chief administrator of the City of Milwaukee, has written wisely about these issues. But I didn't see clearly enough to make the working poor a central theme of the campaign.

In addition to Chip two other young men played key roles. Jimmy Pianka from Erie had an intimate knowledge of Pennsylvania politics, especially the western part of the state, where I was virtually unknown. While Chip busied himself with fund-raising and overall campaign strategy, Jimmy planned particular campaign appearances, making sure that I met the right people – mayors, county chairmen, members of the state committee – and "pressed the flesh" in the Lyndon Johnson style, something I'm not naturally good at. And Jory Tremblay, the young son of friends – his stepfather, Dick Deasy, had succeeded Deb Weiner as my Special Assistant in the Department of Education – functioned as chauffeur, luggage carrier, and factotum – the "Pooh Bah" of the campaign.

After considerable internal debate we decided to locate campaign headquarters in Lancaster. That was convenient for me personally, but unwise from a media point of view; it had the effect of making the campaign nearly invisible to the media in Philadelphia and Pittsburgh, the two major media markets, covering about 40% of the state's population. Nevertheless we rented a suite of rooms on the ground floor of a building in the 300 block of North Duke Street, beginning early in 1979.

The primary opposition did not, at first, appear formidable. It included Craig Lewis, an able if somewhat bombastic state senator from Bucks County; Ed Mezvinsky, a former Congressman from

Iowa, later state chairman of the Democratic Party of Pennsylvania; Peter Liacouras, then Dean of Temple University Law School, later President of the University; C. DeLores Tucker, an African American woman who had been Secretary of State in Shapp's cabinet; Joseph Rhodes, Jr., a thoughtful African American legislator from Pittsburgh; Tom Anderson of Delaware County; and John L. Logue, a political gadfly on the faculty of Villanova University. None of the candidates had much money or statewide recognition; I doubt that any of us could have been identified in the beginning by more than 5% of the likely primary voters. So the race was wide open at that point.

Money was a continuing problem. Alan Hunt, a friend from Swarthmore days and partner in a major Philadelphia law firm, agreed to serve as campaign treasurer. I opened a line of credit in the amount of $100,000 on the security of our two farms at the People's Bank of Oxford, Pennsylvania, where my father had done his banking for nearly 50 years. I importuned family and friends, many of whom gave generously. Chip had me on the telephone nearly every day soliciting contributions. But it was hard work, and after meeting payroll and other immediate expenses we never accumulated enough of a surplus to be able to think about polling or TV.

Pennsylvania is a large and diverse state, which James Carville once memorably described as "Philadelphia, Pittsburgh, and a lot of Alabama in between." I assumed that Lewis, Liacouras, Mezvinsky, et al. would monopolize the Philadelphia area vote, so we planned to spend a lot of time in western Pennsylvania, which had at this point no obvious "favorite son" (or daughter), but where the turnout in Democratic primaries is usually higher than in the rest of the state.

We drove several thousand miles between April 1979 and February 1980. To the Potato City Motor Inn, in Bradford County, where the crowd was small but enthusiastic. To the Bright Hope Baptist Church in Philadelphia, whose pastor, Rev. William Gray, later a Congressman and head of the United Negro Scholarship Fund, was thought to be a key to the black vote in Philadelphia. To a Democratic banquet in heavily Democratic Westmoreland County, where Pianka said, "I won't let you out of this room until you have shaken every hand in it." To Erie, where I had never been.   I also spent a good deal of time with individuals, either potential major contributors or people who were likely to exercise influence with major blocs of Democratic voters; Dick Doran was especially helpful in lining up interviews in the Philadelphia area. People were polite, but mostly non-committal – another warning sign I chose to ignore.

The primary was scheduled for May 1980. The Democratic State Committee met in February to endorse candidates for the Senate and other statewide offices. I had no hope of corralling an endorsement; the best I could hope for was to prevent anyone else from getting the nod.

At the very last minute we were dealt a devastating blow in the form of an announcement by Peter Flaherty, the Democratic Mayor of Pittsburgh, that he was throwing his hat into the ring. Flaherty was a self-styled populist who made much of his affection for the little guy and went out of his way to thumb his nose at major institutions such as banks and the University of Pittsburgh. In 1974 he had run for the United States Senate against Richard Schweiker for the seat being vacated by Hugh Scott, getting 45.9% of the vote. In 1978, he defeated both Bob Casey, then Auditor General, and Ernie Kline, Shapp's Lieutenant Governor, for the Democratic nomination for governor, but could get only 46.4% of the vote against Dick Thornburgh in the fall.

Had Flaherty planned to enter the race all along? I suspect so. Or he might have been enticed by the relative weakness of the field and the absence of any other candidate with a strong base in western Pennsylvania. It made little difference whether or not he was endorsed by the state committee (he wasn't); he was clearly, in terms of both name recognition and ability to raise money, a giant among pygmies.

We didn't need much discussion amongst ourselves to conclude that with Flaherty's candidacy my own had become hopeless. On the last possible day we filed to have my name removed from the primary ballot, and so a quixotic campaign came to an inglorious end. Flaherty easily won the primary in May, getting 53% of the vote against the remaining Democratic candidates, and then went on to lose the general election to Dick Thornburgh, polling 48% of the vote. He later served two terms as County Commissioner of Allegheny County.

I suspect that no matter how intelligently I had organized my campaign, Flaherty's candidacy would have knocked me out of the box. But in order to be taken seriously, I would have had to alter the script in these ways:

1. I should have had a much clearer idea about why I was running, one having nothing to do with my "qualifications" and everything to do with how I intended to use the power of a United States Senator to benefit the people of Pennsylvania.

2. I should have begun, not later than 1971, when I became Secretary of Education, to make lists of people along the lines of "Friends of Bill and Hillary," who could be helpful in a state-wide race; these could have been molded into an effective statewide organization, but it would have taken more time and effort than I was willing to expend at that point in my life.

3. Spending my sabbatical at Harvard was a really dumb thing to do, as it took me out of Pennsylvania for 18 crucial months before the primary. I should have tried to obtain a similar position at the University of Pennsylvania, where at the invitation of Martin Meyerson, the President, I had spent two very pleasant weeks as a "politician in residence" in 1975, or at the University of Pittsburgh.

4. I should have determined at the beginning how much of my own money to invest in the campaign, and stuck with that figure. As things turned out I was forced to sell one of the two farms to pay my campaign debts.

Modern American politics is a strange business. A half century ago the Daley machine in Chicago could pluck Adlai Stevenson, a

Chicago lawyer, out of relative obscurity and make him Governor of Illinois. But political parties have lost that capacity over the past fifty years. Nowadays, to win a statewide race in a large and diverse state like Pennsylvania, you need either broad name recognition, and generally favorable ratings from those who know you, or lots of money with which to buy name recognition. I had neither statewide name recognition nor the money to buy it and thus was probably doomed from the beginning.

Why didn't I pay more attention to the visibly lukewarm enthusiasm of some of my close friends in Lancaster? I suspect because I had, at least subconsciously, set my heart, years ago, on being either a governor or senator; and when an opportunity, in the form of an open U.S. Senate seat, presented itself, I was not to be deterred by practical considerations.

So from a rational point of view my run for statewide office was a mistake; it consumed part of my patrimony and a year and a half of my life. But there were compensations. I came to appreciate the complexity and diversity of Pennsylvania, and I ended up with a new respect for the people in both parties who subject themselves to the rigors of a statewide campaign; whether they win or lose they deserve our admiration, not our contempt.

Chapter 12 - Academic Politics

The spring of 1980 thus found me once more unemployed. In November of that year I proposed marriage to Pauline Leet, Director of the College Center at Franklin and Marshall College, and had the great good fortune to be accepted. We had known each other since 1963 when she and her first husband came to Lancaster. We were married at the President's House on January 10, 1981 and spent our honeymoon at the Caneel Bay Resort on St. John's in the Virgin Islands. My marriage was the best decision I ever made.

Since I was unemployed, and had long since sold my own Lancaster house, I moved in with Pauline, Josiah (18), Matthew (16), Sally (a dog) and Judy (a cat). Josiah decamped the next September for Indiana University of Pennsylvania and, a year later, for the West Coast; Matthew followed him to California after taking some courses at the Camden campus of Rutgers and spending a year and a half in Berlin. So we became a household of two – four, counting Judy and Sally – and I began looking seriously for a job.

One curious episode occurred that spring. In April Keith Spalding, the President of Franklin and Marshall College, called me in some embarrassment – would I be willing to give the principal address at the college commencement and receive an honorary degree? Someone else, after agreeing to be the chief pontificator, had pulled out at the last minute. I agreed and drafted a talk on federalism, which at 17 minutes was twice too long (at Lehigh, in 1973, I did it in 10 minutes – but the intervening years had given me a heightened sense of my own wisdom). To make matters worse, it began to rain halfway through my oration.

Pauline was beginning to think that she might have to support me for the rest of our lives when we received the welcome news that I had been recommended to Ed Blaustein, President of Rutgers University and a former law professor himself, to be Dean of the Rutgers Law School in Camden, New Jersey. (There is another Rutgers University Law School in Newark.) An interview with the President in New Brunswick resulted in a job offer which I readily accepted. We thought about living in Philadelphia and commuting to work across the Ben Franklin Bridge, but Blaustein made it clear that the Dean of a public university law school should live in the state served by his school. So we sold Pauline's Lancaster house and bought one in Riverton, New Jersey, a charming town full of Victorian houses about fives miles north of Camden on the Delaware River, moving there in the summer of 1981.

Being Dean of a law school involved politics of a another sort; although the context was different, the essential task was the same: how to forge acceptable compromises out of very different views. But I was slow to figure that out, and therefore less effective than I might have been.

I have always had, and still have, a certain reverence for the law. I am grateful to have been born and brought up in a country where it is not fatuous to talk about the rule of law, however biased in conception and skewed in application that law may be. As a legislator and legislative secretary to the Governor I had been deeply involved in making laws and as Secretary of Education I was equally involved in their application. Why not spend some time helping a faculty think about the law and educating students to make the legal system work?

I knew by now that people are strongly motivated by self-interest, so I was prepared to deal with a faculty that was deeply interested in salaries, teaching loads, schedules, travel grants and the other perquisites of academic life. These are perfectly natural concerns. What I was not prepared for, though I should have been, was a faculty in love with doctrine. I inherited from Dean Russell Fairbanks a faculty that was divided largely, if not exclusively, along ideological lines. Pat Moynihan used to say that the reason academic politics is so bitter is that the stakes are so small. I would put the matter a bit differently: faculty politics is sometimes bitter because the differences are often ideological ones that don't leave much room for compromise.

In the governmental world – the world of City Hall, Harrisburg and Washington – public officials are forced by the demands of governing to make compromises. A legislator, for example, who takes rigid positions again and again is likely to be seen by his constituents as ineffective, and can be sent packing. There are no similar pressures on the tenured members of a law (or any other) faculty. They can take doctrinaire positions and lose vote after vote in faculty meetings – and nothing happens. There are no forces saying, "Look, we've got to work out a solution that is tolerably satisfactory to everyone or we can't survive."

It is worth noting that we are seeing an increasing amount of ideological behavior on the part of members of Congress and state legislators. Reapportionment deserves some of the blame. The tendency in reapportionment – natural, if unwise – is to strengthen incumbents of both parties vis a vis the other major party, and thus make them vulnerable only to a strong primary opponent. The further result is to pull Republican incumbents to the right and Democratic ones to the left, since those are the directions from which strong primary challenges are likely to come. Compromise becomes more difficult and civil discourse a victim of ideological passions.

During my tenure as Dean the Rutgers/Camden law faculty consisted basically of two factions. One was associated with a movement called Critical Legal Studies. These professors challenged, in their writing and teaching, the prevailing view of law as a neutral, objective system of societal rules. Rather, they argued that the legal system and its rules were politically driven, favored the powerful and dominant classes, and were used by them to maintain their favored position. On the other side were a group of faculty, less cohesive but equally vehement in their views, who rejected just about all the premises from which the Crits operated, being largely content with things as they were. I will call them conservatives.

Hiring and tenure were, of course, the chief battlegrounds. Rutgers instructed us that in making promotion and tenure decisions we were to be guided by three criteria: scholarship, teaching and public service. My impression was that the more conservative faculty, whatever their rhetoric, were in fact weighting these criteria as follows: scholarship – 7; teaching – 2; public service – 1. In their view, bad teaching could disqualify an otherwise acceptable candidate, but even superb teaching could never compensate for mediocre scholarship. The Crits I estimate to have been weighting these criteria as follows: scholarship – 5; teaching – 3; public service – 2. And there were differences in the way each camp judged scholarship: the Crits were more eclectic, willing to consider writing that strayed far from the conventional analyses of constitutions, statutes and common law. The conservatives had a narrower range of vision. These differences led to some hotly contested promotion and tenure decisions, and bad feelings all around.

Grading was also a bone of contention. The conservatives were outraged at the liberal grades given in courses taught by the Crits, and suggested that the Dean make a study of faculty grading patterns with a view to reining in some of their colleagues. The Crits opposed such a move on the grounds that it interfered with faculty autonomy; furthermore, if such a study were undertaken they believed that the resulting grading patterns ought to be made available to students. This the conservatives strongly objected to as an invitation to students to make curriculum decisions for the wrong reasons. In the end we compromised: the study was made, but the results were available to students only in the form of the median grade in each course and no attempt was made to force faculty to adhere to any particular model in the distribution of grades.

Even admissions policy was sometimes a source of controversy. The conservatives looked chiefly at grades and LSAT scores, paying relatively little attention to racial and other factors; the Crits would have cast a wider net. So appointments to the Admissions Committee had to be made in such a way as to balance these competing forces.

In these circumstances what I should have done was to build a "third force," a group of faculty who were neither Crits nor dyed-in-the-wool conservatives, to mediate between the two camps. But I was slow in coming to this conclusion, and clumsy in my efforts to do so. Although my head told me that all things are political, in my heart I still made an exception for colleges and universities. Seduced by visions of Swarthmore College under Frank Aydelotte in the 1930s, I believed that faculty were rational people who would behave civilly to one another and have a high degree of loyalty to the institution.

In fact, many members of the law faculty felt very little loyalty to Rutgers University or to the law school itself. It was like pulling hens' teeth to get some of the faculty to attend graduation or to get even token participation in alumni events and phonathons. One senior member of the faculty was quite candid: "I was hired to teach and write law review articles, not to attend these Mickey Mouse things." So appeals to institutional loyalty didn't carry much weight.

Students were by and large a pleasure to deal with and I found much to admire about them. Many were the first in their family to attend college, let alone professional school. Most had part-time jobs, often exceeding the fifteen hours per week permitted under faculty regulations which I didn't work very hard to enforce. I had a special affection for students in the evening school, many of whom were juggling a fulltime job, evening school four nights a week and family responsibilities. Some of the faculty would cheerfully have abandoned the evening school ("prestigious law schools don't have them") but this would have incurred the wrath of the legislature, and so was politically impossible.

Of course there were disagreements. In 1972 I vetoed the third-year students' choice of Rodney Dangerfield as a graduation speaker; we settled on Judge Leon Higginbotham, a distinguished African American judge on the Third Circuit Court of Appeals, and established a precedent for the Dean and the graduating class having a mutual veto over the choice of a graduation speaker. (The mutual veto is an excellent device, politically, forcing compromise where it might not otherwise be attainable). When I declined to bar military recruiters from the Law School the Gay and Lesbian Rights Association marched in a circle underneath my window chanting, "Pitt, Pitt, full of shit." And the Women's Law Caucus made me promise never to tell again a story, probably apocryphal, about Winston Churchill and Lady Astor, that they deemed sexist. But these were trivial incidents, and it is with a good deal of satisfaction that I now read about the exploits of our graduates who have gone on to distinguished careers at the bar, on the bench and in public service.

I don't mean to give the impression that these disputes absorbed all of our energies. In spite of them we managed to accomplish a good deal in my five years as Dean. We created concentrations in tax and international law, areas in which our faculty and library holdings were particularly strong. We established an exchange program with the law faculty of Karl Francis University in Graz, Austria. We persuaded the university to build a law school dormitory, essential to our ability to attract and keep students in otherwise desperate Camden. We began to raise money systematically outside the university budget. And, of course, the faculty continued to publish, including some first-rate work, and to teach students, on the whole very well. Nonetheless, I was dispirited by having to referee these continuing quarrels, and so, in April of my fourth year, I drove up the New Jersey Turnpike to New Brunswick and handed my resignation to the Provost. I agreed to stay on as Dean for the academic year 1985-86, while the faculty searched for a successor, and the President was kind enough to give me a leave of absence for the Spring semester of 1987 so that I could prepare to teach fulltime, having been given a tenured professorship at the time of my hiring in 1981.

My last eight years at the law school were relatively tranquil and gave me a more benign view of both faculty and students. I taught several courses, mostly Legislation, my favorite; Legal Problems in Education, a natural; and a seminar on Federalism which I thought was intellectually challenging, but my students found somewhat baffling ("who cares which level of government tackles a particular problem" was the prevailing view.) I also chaired important committees such as Appointments, and Promotion and Tenure. When I asked plaintively of one of my successors why I had been chosen to chair what I knew would be contentious committee, he replied: "Because you're the only person everybody trusts." It would have been nice to have seen a bit more of that trust during my years as Dean, but you have to earn it and apparently I hadn't.

Chapter 13 - The State Board of Education

I wasn't, as it turned out, quite finished with Pennsylvania politics, although my next involvement took a new form.

Bob Casey, Sr., a Democrat from Scranton and my former political ally (see Chapter 6), had been elected governor in 1986 over William Warren Scranton, Jr., son of the former Republican governor, by a narrow margin after an unpleasant campaign. His first appointment as Secretary of Education, announced while Pauline and I were on sabbatical in England, was Thomas Gilhool, a Philadelphia lawyer who had won a nationwide reputation litigating issues relating to the education of the handicapped. It was an odd choice. Casey was in many ways a rather conservative man; Gilhool was nothing if not flamboyant. When I was Secretary he had threatened to sue me personally unless I agreed to provide a free public education to all handicapped Pennsylvanians until the age of 21 – something I thought I lacked the legal authority to do. In the view of many, he continued to see the Department as "the enemy," even after he became its chief. When news of the appointment, in the form of an anonymous newspaper clipping, reached us in England, I predicted to Pauline that he would not last two years; he beat my guess by four months.

Gilhool was succeeded by a more conventional choice, Don Carroll, who had been my Deputy Secretary from 1972 to 1975 and then, after a spell as a private consultant, Superintendent of the

Harrisburg school system, a thankless job (the district has recently been taken over by the state). Secretary Carroll began a quiet campaign to have me appointed to the State Board of Education. The appointment finally came through in 1991 for a term ending in 1996; I became not only a member of the Board, but chairman of its Council on Higher Education, one of the two principal working arms of the Board.

The Board had undergone one major transformation since I had last been acquainted with its work. Under the terms of a statute passed during the Thornburg Administration one member from each of the four caucuses of the General Assembly was to serve on the Board. Although they could not vote on final passage of policy matters, they were otherwise free to take an active role in the Board's work. There had been talk of such a move when I was Secretary: I had made it clear privately that I was opposed to such a bill and would probably resign if it passed.

In my judgment putting legislators on the Board was both unwise and possibly unconstitutional. It was unwise because the legislative members tended to bully their colleagues, threatening to undo the Board's work when it came before the General Assembly for review. This had the effect of depriving the Board of its objective non-partisan character, which was the whole point of its existence. It was quite possibly unconstitutional on separation of powers grounds. Regrettably, I think legislative membership on the Board is here to stay, a monument to the continuing wars between the two political branches. I once remonstrated with a legislative member of the Board who, in my judgment and that of several of my colleagues, was abusing his position, only to be told that if we made a fuss he would simply introduce legislation to abolish the Board. He knew, and I knew, that such legislation would probably pass, the Board having no political base and consequently very few friends in the General Assembly.

I know when the practice of putting legislators, or their surrogates, on boards and commissions in the executive branch began, because I was, to borrow Dean Acheson's phrase, "present at the creation." In 1971, while I was still legislative secretary to the governor, a Democratic state senator begged Governor Shapp to name him to the board of trustees of the local state college – "I have a tough election coming up, and it will be a feather in my cap." I argued against setting what I thought was an unwise precedent; once on the boards, legislators would meddle in personnel decisions and complicate the lives of college presidents in many other ways. But I was overruled. Now the practice is endemic, at least in the Department of Education. At first the appointments were optional with the governor, but increasingly statutes began to require legislative appointments, sometimes of legislators themselves, sometimes of their "designees."

Why did a series of otherwise intelligent men – Shapp, Thornburgh, Casey, and Ridge – acquiesce so meekly in the weakening of an important gubernatorial prerogative? For the same reason, I suspect, that every President since Franklin Roosevelt has signed bills containing a legislative veto, an equally pernicious practice. No sensible president or governor will incur a clear and present danger, the wrath of the legislature, in order to avoid a speculative and future one, the erosion of the chief executive's authority. All the more reason for the courts to patrol this boundary line with special vigor.

My first two years on the Board were dominated by a raucous statewide debate about "outcome-based" education. Secretary Carroll had persuaded Governor Casey that instead of judging public education in terms of "inputs" (Carnegie units, dollars per child, books per child) we should measure what children had actually learned, what they "knew and were able to do." Good in theory, but difficult in practice. Extremists on the radical right seized on some unwise language in early drafts of the proposed "outcomes" document to argue that the Board was intent on brainwashing children, negating parental influence, and undermining religious belief. This charge, though spurious, was taken up by the religious right all over the country. Governor Casey distanced himself from the ensuing fracas, leaving the Board and Secretary Carroll to dangle in the wind. Eventually the succeeding Ridge Administration, by the clever device (among other things) of calling the proposed goals "performance-based" instead of "outcomes-based," was able to get a set of regulations through both the Board and the legislature establishing standards and requiring testing of reading, writing, and mathematics in the 5th, 8th, and 11th grades. The whole episode convinced me, if I needed convincing, that in politics, appearances trump realities; once significant numbers of people, including some in the press who should have known better, began to believe that the Board was up to some witchcraft, it was all over.

Midway though my term on the Board Tom Ridge, a Republican Congressman from Erie, had been elected governor. He nominated as Secretary of Education Eugene Hickok, an assistant professor of political science from nearby Dickinson College with close ties to the Heritage Foundation and other conservative institutions (until recently the Number 2 person in President George W. Bush's Department of Education). On the basis of Ridge's voting record in Washington we expected him to be a moderate in the style of Governor Scranton, but we were wrong, at least where education policy was concerned.

Hickok made it clear from the beginning that he had nothing but contempt for the State Board, which in his view was part of the same education establishment that was responsible for the so-called failure of the public schools. The administration therefore bypassed the Board whenever it could; for at least two years the Board was reduced to reviewing proposed regulations under various state and federal statutes, a useful but not very exciting exercise. But after ignoring the Board the Ridge Administration apparently decided that it could be a useful instrument after all, so they set about stacking the Board with like-minded people. Most previous governors had been careful to make bi-partisan appointments, but Ridge had a different slant on things, and by the end of the Ridge Administration there were no Democrats on the Board.

The Ridge Administration also chose to make vouchers its flagship educational issue. Democrats suspected that this was Ridge's strategy for wooing the religious right as a way of transforming himself into a viable candidate for national office. If so, the strategy was a failure. On three separate occasions a voucher bill reached the point where a vote by the House of Representatives would have been in order; on all three occasions the Republican House leadership pulled the bill, apparently lacking a constitutional majority. (Rumors were to the effect that they were at least seven votes short of the 102 that would have been required under the Pennsylvania Constitution).

Those defeats did not prevent the Ridge Administration from attempting to funnel financial assistance to private schools in other ways. In 2001 Governor Ridge, just before leaving for Washington to become Czar of Homeland Security, obtained passage of a bill creating certain state tax credits for corporations; eighty percent of the credits were set aside for corporations which paid tuition for children who, being enrolled in a failing public school, chose to attend another public or a private school. More recently, under Governor Mark Schweiker, who succeeded to the job when Ridge went to Washington, the state has taken over the Philadelphia public schools, assigning a major role in some 20 schools to the Edison Corporation; while not a voucher program this effort stems from the same animus toward the public schools that lies behind vouchers.

My job as Chairman of the Council of Higher Education was an exercise in frustration. The <u>Girard</u> case (see Chapter 7) provided a solid legal base for the Board's authority over public schools K-12, but there was no such consensus about the Board's power to legislate for colleges and universities, even the public ones. As a legislator I had tried to clarify that role during the 1965-66 session, but without success.

Penn State posed the greatest challenge. Not long after I became Chairman of the Council on Higher Education Graham Spanier, the new President of Penn State, announced a plan to expand the university's role by converting some of the seventeen two-year branch campuses to four-year schools. His plan was widely attacked by both public and private institutions, which saw Penn State invading "their" territory. The Board sent a letter to Spanier questioning his authority to act without Board approval, and held public hearings. Eventually Penn State agreed to some largely cosmetic changes in the western part of the state, and the controversy died down.

A similar challenge to the Board's authority came from the Board of Governors of the State System of Higher Education, which under the terms of a 1982 statute supplanted the Department in making policy for the fourteen state colleges, now universities. The Board of Governors proposed adding a doctoral program in physical therapy at Slippery Rock and one in pharmacy at Shippensburg University. The State Board sent a letter to Chancellor James McCormick, questioning his authority, which had the effect of getting Governor Ridge and Secretary Hickok into the act. Eventually the physical therapy program was approved (the pharmacy program having been abandoned), but only after the Board of Governors acknowledged the State Board's authority over issues of program duplication.

The issue with the community colleges was quite the reverse: not how to curb their authority, but how to strengthen their role. Community colleges had been authorized by a statute passed in the George Leader Administration (1955-59), but Pennsylvania botched the job, as it so often does, by diffusing authority in deference to the sacred idol of "local control." Instead of doing what Rockefeller did in New York, and creating a genuine statewide system of public higher education, the legislature authorized the creation of community colleges either by counties or by consortia of school districts. Theoretically costs were to be shared one-third by the sponsoring unit of government, one-third by the state and one-third by the student. This "system," or, more accurately, lack of one, combined with Penn State's aggressiveness in establishing branch campuses, has had several undesirable effects:

1. Some of the more sparsely settled areas of the state are still not served by any two-year public institution;

2. Some areas, like Lancaster County, are served by the branch of a community college located in an adjacent county, resulting in students paying two-thirds rather than one-third of the cost;

3. Some sponsoring authorities have not fulfilled even their one-third obligation, once again adding to student financial burdens; and,

4. The Board has had to deal with a number of petitions from school districts seeking to be added to – or, more frequently,

subtracted from – the roster of sponsoring authorities of a particular community college.

Part of the difficulty lies in the fact that the community colleges speak with a weak voice in Harrisburg. The Council on Higher Education was beginning to grapple with this question as I was leaving the Board in 1996. I wish them well but have no confidence in the outcome.

It would be easy to become cynical about the ambitions of colleges and universities. Instead of doing well what they had been created to do, it seemed to me they were always aspiring to climb to the next level of prestige: two-year colleges sought to become four-year, four-year colleges sought to add graduate programs, institutions with masters degree programs yearned to add doctoral programs or professional schools. Then it occurred to me that I was simply witnessing one more manifestation of a general rule: all human institutions seek to expand until they come up against forces they cannot overcome. This is certainly true of governments, and explains why Madison and his colleagues embraced a federal system and the separation of powers. It is equally true of educational institutions. And that is why the Pennsylvania legislature ought to empower the State Board to umpire quarrels among the various segments of higher education. And it is why this effort continues to fail.

One often hears people (usually educators of one sort or another) say that education should not become a "political football." This is a self-serving notion promoted by the education fraternity in an attempt to insulate its work from interference on the part of governors, legislators, mayors, members of city council and other politicians. But it is wrong-headed. Education is the largest item in most state budgets, as well as the largest area of expenditure for most communities. It is not feasible to keep issues relating to educational taxing and spending out of the public arena. And the debate about education being a "political football" distracts attention from the real questions, such as whether taxes to support education are fair and whether educational practices are wise.

A plausible argument can be made that the State Board of Education should not exist. Unlike the Governor and the General Assembly, it is not accountable to the voters. And unlike the judiciary it performs no functions that absolutely require it to be insulated from public pressures. It does its best work when it carries out policies entrusted to it by the political branches, as, for example, when it presided over the merger of 2,000 school districts into 504 during the 1960s. But the Board needs to understand that it has no political base, and thus must be cautious in its dealings with the governor and the General Assembly.

In the summer of 1996, wanting to occupy the high moral ground, I wrote Governor Ridge a brief letter asking not to be considered for reappointment to the Board. I received by way of reply a perfunctory note from some mid-level bureaucrat, thanking me for my services to the Commonwealth. And so ended another chapter in my political education.

Chapter 14 - "Brighten the Corner Where You Are"

By 1996 Pauline and I had come regretfully to the conclusion that it would be necessary to sell Pittwillow Farm. My arthritis was getting worse, a series of mishaps had fused my backbone into a single inflexible joint, and I was diagnosed as being in the early stages of Parkinson's. I was, as a result, quite useless for heavy work. And although by then we were renting the tillable fields to a neighbor, the burden of planting and tending a large garden, mowing lawns, repairing fences, shoring up a stone farm house built in 1818, and entertaining an endless stream of friends and relatives, was more than I could reasonably ask Pauline to do. And so, with great reluctance, since the farm had been in my family since 1926 and had played an important role in my life, we put it on the market. It took two years to find a buyer, but eventually we did, moving out in the summer of 1997.

There was never much doubt that we would end up back in Lancaster. Pauline had a sentimental attachment to New England, having been born and raised there, but Lancaster made more sense – it was where both of us had spent the bulk of our adult lives, where we had many friends and could fit easily into the life of the community. We visited two retirement communities and settled on Homestead Village, one mile West of the city in East Hempfield Township. They had nothing open for us at the moment, so we spent a year in a nearby apartment building, moving finally to a comfortable ground floor apartment in Homestead in July of 1998.

As soon as we had gotten settled I paid a call on Kay Angermier, the enthusiastic if somewhat disorganized head of the local Democratic Party. She appointed me as the Democratic committeeman for the Barrcrest precinct of East Hempfield Township; then, when we moved to Homestead, as committeeman of the Rohrerstown precinct. (One advantage of there being so many vacancies on the County Committee is that it's usually not hard to fit new people into the existing structure).

My first item of business after obtaining the official list of voters was to ascertain the boundaries of the Barrcrest precinct. Easier said than done! First, I visited the Bureau of Elections in the Courthouse where Karen Axe, whom I had known for 30 years, presided. She explained gently that they no longer had precinct maps, only a computer program that, given a voter's address, assigns the voter to the correct precinct. She suggested that I consult East Hempfield Township. So I drove out to the township building where I was offered a planning commission map – but no precinct boundaries. In desperation I set about making a map from the street list and a commercial map of the area – a laborious process, but then I had few competing claims on my time during the year in Barrcrest.

I then began recruiting a work force. Even a good committeeperson cannot personally cover a whole precinct; my rule of thumb is that you need about one worker for every 30-40 registered voters. A mutual friend, Eileen Wise, widow of Sidney Wise, helped out in Barrcrest

Apartments. Bob Barden, recently retired, became committeeman. A significant find, with repercussions far beyond the precinct, were Judi and Ken Ralph; she became committeewoman, and he served (and still does) as Chairman of the Communications Committee of the County party and performs numerous other tasks beyond the scope of his formal responsibilities.

After we moved to Homestead Village I set about organizing the Democratic Party in the Rohrerstown precinct. This turned out to be surprisingly easy, largely because of Homestead Village itself. Although Democrats at Homestead are outnumbered by about 4-1, most of the 50 or so Democrats are not only dependable voters, but eager to help in other ways as well. So when I issued a call for volunteers I could generally count on 10-15 people for stuffing and addressing envelopes, telephoning Democratic voters the weekend before the election, and staffing the polling place on Election Day. We are proud of the fact that although Democrats are generally, for reasons relating to education and income, less likely than Republicans to vote, in the 2000 presidential election our turnout in the Rohrerstown precinct exceeded theirs by 72% to 68%, a rare occurrence in East Hempfield and in the county generally.

When we moved back to Lancaster County I had a fairly clear picture of what I wanted to do to help strengthen the county party in the next four years. But it all hinged on having a good county chairman – someone who would provide strong leadership while allowing the rest of us some running room. Fortunately for me, and for the Democratic Party as well, a young man named Scott

Brubaker stepped forward, who was close to being the ideal candidate. He had been elected to the Denver Borough Council in his mid-twenties, later becoming its president. Both he and his wife, Jennifer, worked for the Democratic leadership in the House of Representatives in Harrisburg and were thus knowledgeable about state issues. A Marine Corps reservist, deeply religious, skilled at dealing with the press, Scott was the right choice to head the party in this very conservative county. He and I developed a good working relationship; if he was sometimes irritated by my rather free-wheeling activities, he never showed it. His place was taken in 2002 by Bruce Beardsley, a businessman with a very different style of leadership, but equally effective.

Our plans for the county party hinged in part on money. In 1997, we were raising about $10,000 per year in support of our core budget. We had a headquarters, a hole-in-the-wall across from the Courthouse, plus a grungy basement meeting room, but no one was there most of the time, so incoming calls were returned casually or not at all. A viable political party requires a continuing and palpable presence; people need to know where they can call to volunteer, to contribute, or just to bitch. And the greatest sin in politics is not making adequate use of volunteers.

So we set about raising the stakes. Scott asked Janice Stork, the former two-term Democratic Mayor of the City of Lancaster, and me to co-chair the Finance Committee, and Janice and I recruited about 20 others to make ten phone calls each. Those calls were surprisingly productive. It turned out that many Democrats were just waiting to be asked. The party is now – several years later – raising $30,000 annually toward the headquarters budget. We were able to hire a competent part-time Office Manager, Lori Axon, later replaced by Tracy Lynn Arriola; to put out a newsletter four times a year; to buy computerized voter data quarterly from the Bureau of Elections; and in 2001, for the first time, to give not only technical help but modest amounts of money to local candidates who looked as though they had a real chance of winning.

In the process we are educating Lancaster County Democrats about their obligation to the party itself. Occasionally a prospective donor says, "I give only to candidates, not to political parties." We point out that a vibrant party is crucial to successful candidacies. Sometimes we are persuasive, sometimes not. Republicans in Lancaster County are more successful than we have been in persuading their voters to support the party on a regular basis. Of course it doesn't hurt their cause that they monopolize political power in the county; if you want a job or a consulting contract you go to them, not to us. Under the circumstances, it is hardly surprising that their core budget is roughly ten times ours; it is a minor miracle that we survive from one election cycle to the next.

A second area of concern was the failure of our local party to articulate any rationale for voting Democratic. The often-asserted need to create a genuine two-party system, however true, just isn't very persuasive; it appeals to the mind but not to the heart. And because so few Democrats hold public office in the county, there are few people, other than the Minority Commissioner, to sound the themes we regard as quintessentially Democratic. Once again, Scott took the lead, appointing a Policy Committee, which first produced a ten-page statement and then a shorter and snappier brochure. The statement is a bit on the "motherhood and apple pie" side of things, but on the whole it meets our needs; and I assume it will be revised from time to time. It has also been translated into Spanish, a crucial move in a county where the Spanish-speaking population is growing rapidly.

Not long after I became Committeeman in the Rohrerstown precinct I was elected District leader in the Hempfield School District. The county party is organized by school districts, of which there are 17, with the committee people in each district electing a leader for a four-year term. The position in the Hempfield area had been vacant for several years. With 27 precincts, the Hempfield School District should have had 54 committee people; we had on paper exactly seven, and several of them resigned within a year of my taking over. So there was a mammoth recruiting job to do.

The Hempfield School District comprises four municipalities: East Hempfield Township, where I live (16 precincts); West Hempfield Township (7 precincts); East Petersburg Borough (3 precincts), and Mountville Borough (1 precinct). Voter registration was about 19,000 Republicans, 6,000 Democrats, and 2,000 "no party." There were only two Democratic officeholders: Nancy Mc Gee, who had been elected to Borough Council in Mountville, and Kevin Kornfield, who had been appointed to Borough Council in East Petersburg to fill an unexpired term.

I began recruiting committee people in East Hempfield, since that was where I lived, although a good case could be made that I should have begun in West Hempfield, which was not quite so one-sided. My method was simplicity itself. I began with the street list, the official list of registered voters in each precinct. Each county in Pennsylvania decides for itself what information to put on the street list, although this is about to give way, under pressure of federal law, to a uniform state system. Chester County, for example, lists telephone numbers (very helpful) but not voting history (very unhelpful). Lancaster County does the opposite: voting history but, until very recently, no telephone numbers. Voting histories tell you whether or not the voter has gone to the polls in the four most recent elections; thus "NYNY" tells you that the voter in question has voted in two of the last four elections. A more elaborate history, encompassing the past 15 elections, is available in computerized form from the Election Bureau.

The next step was to go through the street list highlighting all the Democrats who had voted in at least three of the past four elections. These were the party stalwarts – the people who voted rain or shine. Unfortunately, many of the staunch Democrats were over 65, their core convictions having been molded by the Depression and World War II. I made a list of these frequent-voting Democrats and looked up their telephone numbers. It is usually possible to obtain phone numbers for at least 80% of them, although the increasing number of households with unlisted numbers is frustrating.

Then came the tricky part – the phone call. I would begin with couples, on the premise that two stalwart Democrats in the same household afforded stronger psychological support for what would be at best a difficult undertaking. I generally introduced myself as follows:

Hi. I'm John Pittenger. You don't know me (occasional protestations to the contrary), but I'm the head of the Democratic Party in the Hempfield School District. I notice that you are not only a registered Democrat, but also that you vote regularly. That's great! Could I stop by your house sometime in the next week or two to talk about how you might help us out in the precinct where you live?

By identifying myself at the very beginning I took some of the edge off what was obviously a "cold" call, and by praising their voting record I presumably created a more receptive mood for my message.

From that point on the conversations diverged. Some said, right off the bat, "sorry, not interested" – although almost no one was rude. For many it was, "I'd be interested, but I have no spare time." Their excuses cast some light on the way Americans live at the beginning of the 21st century. "I have a two hour commute each way to my job." "My husband has Alzheimer's, and I am fully occupied looking after him." "We plan to be in Florida from November through April." "I'm President of the soccer league and coach three teams." Many expressed regret at not being able to help; I made a note to get back in touch with them in a year or two.

Then there are the voters who ask, not unreasonably, "What do you mean by 'help out'"? At this stage, I never mention the words "committee person" – many would have no idea what I was talking about, and others would be frightened away. I don't even mention going door-to-door, as that seems to be a daunting prospect for many. Rather I talk in terms of activities that are relatively non-threatening, like helping with mailings or telephoning Democrats the weekend before the election.

A few people beg off at this point, but more often than not it's, "OK, come on over, I'd at least like to see what a live Democrat looks like in this county." So we make a date. I check to make sure I have their correct address, giving them my phone number in case they want to change the time or date (and, not incidentally, reassuring them that I am a real person).

The interview itself is crucial. There are no fixed rules – I just play it by ear. Sometimes it will be clear from the beginning that the person is unsuitable -- too old, too overwhelmed by small children, too inarticulate. In that case, I bring the interview to a speedy (but, I hope, graceful) conclusion, extracting a promise to "help out when I can." Sometimes I ask for suggestions about who might make a good committeeperson, reading names from the street list. Democrats in the Hempfield Area are almost always surprised by how many of their neighbors are Democrats; they think we're outnumbered by 10-1 rather than 3-1. It is surprising, also, how little suburbanites know about their neighbors; unless they have school-age children they tend to live in isolation from one another, which helps explain the "anomie" or lack of a sense of community which Bellah and others have described in "The Good Society."

If the person strikes me in the first five minutes as potential committee material, I launch into the "sell." It involves a brief sketch of my own political involvement, emphasizing how much I have enjoyed being a committeeperson in three quite different locations. I answer questions – "How much time does it take?" and "What kind of help can I expect?" being the most frequent.

It helps that I have no preconceptions about the sort of person who ought to be committeeperson in a particular precinct. I don't care about gender, race, or church affiliation; I'm chiefly interested in someone who will do the work. Once I recommended someone with a Polish last name to a fellow district leader whose reply was, "that name wouldn't go over in our area." But this misconstrues the nature of the work. It doesn't require speeches, or letters to the editor; it's mostly a matter of communicating with your fellow Democrats, and they tend to be a broad-minded bunch. On another occasion when I was recruiting Election Day callers, the woman on the other end of the telephone said, after a moment's hesitation, "There's one thing you ought to know – I'm an African American." My reply: "So what?" If the Democratic Party can't play a central role in overcoming differences of race, religion, and nationality, we should fold up our tents and leave the field to the prejudiced, of whom there are plenty in Lancaster County.

If the answer is "yes" I offer congratulations and give them some information – a street list, voter registration and absentee ballot forms, a map of the precinct (if we have one) and a schedule of events. The county chairman will follow up with a letter of appointment and other materials, including the by-laws of the County Committee, maps of the various legislative districts, a copy of our county policy statement and a Manual for Committeepersons.

If I am turned down by my first prospect, it's on to the next. In some precincts I have hit pay dirt on the first call; in some I have spent two years and made 20 calls without recruiting anyone. When I have exhausted the 4Y and 3Y Democrats, I go on to the 2Ys. In a place like the Hempfield School District, which has been uncompetitive for so many years, Democrats don't have a very powerful motive to vote, especially in odd-numbered years when only county and municipal offices are at stake, so there is nothing inherently ridiculous about looking for prospective committee people among people who vote less often.

Sometimes I am too persuasive for my own good. Although we now have filled about 40 of the 54 committee slots in the Hempfields I have recruited and then lost another 25 or so. Sometimes they come to their senses the next day, calling apologetically. Sometimes it takes a week or month. The excuses vary – "my husband disapproves;" "my doctor is against it;" "I've taken a more demanding job;" "I've decided I'm just too shy." I never argue, and try to conceal my disappointment, thanking them for being willing to consider it and expressing the hope that they will help "as circumstances allow." There may be a less arduous way to recruit committee people; if so, I hope someone will tell me about it.

Are Robert Putnam and others right in seeing a marked decline in civic engagement on the part of the American people? On the surface, the fact that we were able to recruit 40 committee people in three years suggests that their fears are exaggerated. But perhaps not. Our successes in the Hempfields have, by and large, not been replicated in other parts of the county. At the present time the Democratic Party doesn't exist in about a third of the county's 225 precincts and has only a nominal existence in another third. Only in about 75 precincts, mostly in Lancaster City, Lancaster Township, Columbia Borough, Manheim Township, and the Hempfields does the party have a vigorous presence.

It is encouraging to note that many people who are asked to contribute to or work for the local Democratic Party ultimately say, "Yes." It might seem that we are limited chiefly by the number of people who can be persuaded to make the necessary phone calls. But there's the rub: as soon as you start talking about assuming responsibility, people suddenly become very shy. They are willing to tackle the mundane chores – distributing leaflets and stuffing envelopes – but they don't want the responsibility of organizing an entire precinct. So in more than one precinct I have found myself in the situation of having plenty of volunteers but no one to coordinate their activities – Indians, but no chiefs. Perhaps Putnam is right after all.

What have our 40 committee people been able to accomplish in the past several years?

We began 1999 with a stroke of good luck. A small notice in the daily press advertised the fact that the Hempfield Area School District was soliciting applications from citizens interested in filling a vacancy on the School Board. The district furnished me with the names and addresses of the applicants; to my astonishment it turned out that six of the eleven were registered Democrats (the Board naturally appointed one of the Republican applicants). I got in touch with the six and ascertained that two of them, Barbara Zimmerman, a nursing professor at Millersville University, and Tom Arnold, a city fireman, were interested in running for the full four-year term in the fall. So we circulated petitions and, as Pennsylvania law permits, filed them in both party primaries. By the luck of the draw Barbara won first place on the Republican primary ballot. Largely because of this, her own hard work, and the fact that Republicans were focusing on bitter primary contests for several county offices, she won both primaries and thus was effectively unopposed in the fall. Tom fared less well, winning only the Democratic primary, and losing by the usual 2-1 margin in November. I was widely, and incorrectly, credited with Barbara's election. But I have learned in politics that since you will be blamed for events over which you have no control, you might as well take credit for your serendipitous victories.

The year 2000 presented a different set of challenges. Only federal and state offices were on the ballot so we were in the position of supporting candidates in whose selection we had played little or no role. The exception was the 37th State House seat, which included all of the Hempfield area. The four-term Republican incumbent declined to run for re-election, pursuant to a self-imposed four-term limit, leading to a messy five-way Republican primary battle. An active Republican, Deb Hayes, changed parties to run as a Democrat, taking an unpaid leave from her civil service job to do so. She lost badly but deserves great credit for "showing the flag."

We are not likely, in the foreseeable future, to carry Lancaster County or the Hempfield Area School District in national or state elections. But as I keep telling our committee people, sometimes you "win," not by winning big, but by losing small. The 2000 election is a case in point. As the Philadelphia suburbs have become more Democratic the state Republican Party has had to rely increasingly on Lancaster and other "Dutch" counties for statewide pluralities. In 2000 their Lancaster county chairman predicted that Bush would carry the county by 90,000 votes. In the event, his local margin was only 61,000 and he lost the state by 200,000. Thus, we made a major contribution to Al Gore's victory in Pennsylvania, only to find our efforts nullified by the travesty in Florida. Admittedly, it is more inspiring to say, "Let's win," rather than, "Let's lose by fewer than 90,000." But it has to be clear to a committeeperson that if she succeeds in cutting the normal Republican plurality in her precinct from 500-200 to 450-250 she is making a major contribution to the fortunes of the party at all levels.

In 2001 I stepped down as District Leader in the Hempfields to devote more time to the county party. My place was taken by Bruce Marks, a retired engineer, a delightful colleague and someone who was computer-literate as I was not. When Bruce died tragically two years later we elected Martin Dees, Jr., a retired Armstrong Cork Company chemist, to take his place, which Martin has done with enthusiasm.

Under the Pennsylvania Election calendar 2001 was another county and local year. There were 21 offices to be filled in the four municipalities constituting the Hempfield Area School District. We were able to field candidates for only five of the 21 positions, but that represented a substantial advance on 1997, the last comparable year. Even though we won only one of the five contests, the outcomes were, on the whole, encouraging.

In East Petersburg Borough, where three council seats were being contested, Todd Weiss, a Democrat, finished third out of four candidates and thus won a seat on the council. He benefited from the fact that one of the three Republican primary victors had moved out of town, a fact the Republicans discovered too late to have him removed from the ballot, so they attempted to write-in a third Council candidate. Todd had a good issue, the Borough Council having been, in the eyes of many residents, less than candid the previous year about attempts to locate a probation and parole office in the Borough, a move widely opposed. He was also an energetic and an effective candidate. When the smoke cleared Todd had beaten the write-in candidate by 167 votes – in East Petersburg, a landslide. And in West Hempfield Township Bonnie Capcara ran an energetic and almost successful campaign for township supervisor, garnering about 45% of the vote, almost double what two nominal Democrats had achieved two years before.

The moral of all this is quite easy to decipher: with good candidates and an energetic campaign, Democrats can win local elections in Lancaster County. Not every time, or even a majority of the time, but often enough to create the two-party system which is essential to a healthy democracy.

The year 2002 was a federal and state election year highlighted by the race for governor. Tom Ridge, Pennsylvania's Republican governor, had been summoned to Washington to head up the Homeland Security Office, and his successor, Lieutenant Governor Mark Schweiker, disclaimed any interest in running himself. The Attorney General, Mike Fisher, emerged as the only plausible Republican candidate. Democrats, on the other hand, had to get through a bitter primary contest between Ed Rendell, the charismatic ex-mayor of Philadelphia, and Bob Casey, Jr., Auditor General and son of the former governor. Rendell prevailed, but we worried that the mean-spirited primary conducted by Casey had damaged Rendell's appeal in the Fall. We need not have been concerned – Ed was spectacular, both as a campaigner and a fund-raiser, and beat Fisher by 300,000 votes in November. In Lancaster County, it was another case of "winning big by losing small." The Republican County chairman predicted a Fisher plurality of 70,000; this time it was only 43,000, not nearly enough to overcome Rendell's huge majorities in Philadelphia and its suburbs.

Legislative reapportionment following the 2000 census had created a new House seat, the 41st, which we agreed it would be a dereliction in duty not to contest in 2002. I took charge of the effort to recruit a suitable candidate. I was interviewing Robert Achtermann, a retired minister, when half-way through our conversation he said, "You know, you are interviewing the wrong member of this family; my wife would make a much better candidate." So I returned the next day to interview Barbara, who to my delight finally said, "Yes." She was retiring on June 30 from a distinguished 35-year career as a teacher, social worker, and counselor in Lancaster County. I didn't conceal from her the fact that it would be an uphill battle – only if everything broke in our favor would we have an outside chance – and she agreed to give it her best try.

Having persuaded Barbara to run I felt obligated to help out, and thus became her campaign coordinator. We had an amateurish but dedicated campaign committee; working with them and with Barbara was a real pleasure. And although we raised almost $10,000 and Barbara rang about 1,500 doorbells, and made good use of both direct mail and radio, she lost in the end by 13,371 to 6,530, which was still an improvement on past performance. Rendell's coattails, which we had been counting on, proved non-existent.

It is increasingly difficult to recruit candidates in what are essentially one-party districts. If you paint too rosy a picture of the possibilities you run the risk of demoralizing a good person, perhaps turning them off to the political process altogether. But if you paint a totally frank picture of the prospects you run the risk of not having a candidate. I did my best to steer between these two rocks; but the fact that 83 Pennsylvania House candidates were essentially unopposed in the 2002 general election suggests the dimensions of the problem.

In 2003 we were involved once again in a county and local election year. We nominated candidates for seven of the twenty-one local offices at stake. Barbara Zimmerman, running for re-election to the School Board, appeared on Election Night to have lost the Republican primary, and thus any real prospect of success in November, by 2,091 to 2,088; but when Martin Dees and I went down to Voter Services the following week to monitor the recount, she picked up 7 votes in the Rohrerstown precinct and was declared the winner by 2,095 to 2,091. In November, Barbara, again running on both tickets, won overwhelmingly, polling 400 votes more than the nearest Republican. John Wennerholt won an uncontested election for Auditor in East Hempfield. Tony Crocamo, running for Supervisor against the Republican County Chairman in West Hempfield, gained a creditable 40% of the vote. Two other candidates lost by wider margins.

One of the small triumphs of the past few years in the Hempfield area has been the formation of a Democratic Club at Hempfield High School. It owes its continuing existence largely to one man, Dr. George Leyh, a social studies teacher who was twice an unsuccessful Democratic candidate for the state House. Student enthusiasm alone won't sustain such an effort – the turnover is too rapid. But we have managed to recruit 10-12 students each year (55 in 2004!) to conduct voter registration drives in the high school, debate their Republican classmates, help committee people with leafleting and take occasional trips to Harrisburg or Washington. One entirely unanticipated benefit has been to draw the parents of some of the students into local politics as well; I count at least five current committee people who were in essence recruited by their sons and daughters.

I am not the least bit surprised that students have taken so readily to politics. Unlike much of what they study in school (however important in laying the foundation for further studies or a career) politics is in some sense real, a way of connecting to the adult world that they yearn to be part of. And it seems to me that political experience ought to be built into the curriculum itself rather than left to the hope that a Dr. Leyh will emerge in every high school in the state; at some point in the past 25 years we seem to have stopped teaching civics in our public schools.

Sometimes I think that the most useful thing I have done politically is to bring young people into the mainstream of political life. My accomplishments as a legislator, as legislative staff and as Secretary of Education are hardly memorable. But in recruiting dozens of young (and not so young) women and men, Republicans as well as Democrats, to a more positive view of the political process, and a willingness to engage themselves in it, I think I have done a public service. Oliver Wendell Holmes, Jr. once wrote: "You must share in the action and passion of your time, or live at the peril of being judged not to have lived." I think I've done that, and enticed others to do it as well.

One of the conclusions to be drawn from my admittedly eclectic career is that a person can derive satisfaction from participating in politics at any level. Few will have the resources or stamina for a state-wide campaign in a state of twelve million people. Even a congressional seat (pop. – 620,000), or one in the State Senate (pop. – 250,000) or State House (pop. – 60,000) will be beyond the grasp of many, at least without the organization and resources of a strong political party – and as we have seen, these are a diminishing presence. But borough and township races in Lancaster County involve at the most 10,000 voters, and in some of the smaller municipalities you can win with fewer than 1,000 votes. So you can play the game at whatever level is consistent with your time, energy and resources; after all, most major league baseball players began their careers in the minor leagues. But it takes people at all levels, in both parties, in a wide variety of roles, to make the system work.

Chapter 15 - Endings

So what have I learned from 45 years of political activity – almost all of it, admittedly, in Pennsylvania, but encompassing a wide variety of positions, state and local, appointed and elected, public and party? In particular, have the preconceptions with which I entered political life been altered by these experiences? And if so, in what directions?

Self-interest, including my own, plays a much larger role than I was willing to concede as a young man; reason and compassion are less powerful forces than I could have hoped. Why this should be so – whether it is the product of a long evolutionary process emphasizing survival as the prize, or other forces – makes, for my purposes, no difference; it is simply a fact. In analyzing people's motives for conduct in public life, whether it be legislators enhancing their chances of reelection by gerrymandering their districts or voters in East Petersburg fighting to prevent a Probation and Parole office from being located in their borough, self-interest is a dominant motive.

In emphasizing the role of self-interest in politics I am not, however, putting forward a counsel of despair.

In the first place, people do have consciences – some strong, others weak. We need to do all we can to strengthen the role of conscience, the "other regarding" side of our natures. But many people of goodwill are politically ineffective because they operate from premises like the ones that encumbered me at the outset of my political life. They search for ideal solutions, and when these seem unattainable, they lose heart, abandoning public life altogether: a classic case of the best being enemy to the good.

Ralph Nader's followers provide a case study of this mentality at work. If you tax a Nader enthusiast with having cost Gore the 2000 presidential election by siphoning off votes which would mostly have gone to Gore, you generally get one of three rejoinders: (1) denial, i.e., the assertion that Nader did not draw more votes from Gore than from Bush (I take it this is Nader's position); or (2) an assertion, less plausible in 2004, that since Bush and Gore are "peas in a pod" it didn't make any difference who occupied the White House; or (3) an avowal that since Nader was "right" on the issues, a vote for him was a "principled" vote, the consequences be damned.

It is this third position that chiefly interests me. I suspect it is connected to the strain of utopianism in much American Protestant thought, a utopianism that persists even today although Reinhold Niebuhr demolished its intellectual foundations more than fifty years ago. Perhaps I can help persuade some of these people of goodwill the futility of their position and the need to remain engaged, even when the choices are unpalatable; politics is, after all, the art of the possible.

For a larger number of voters self-interest will always be the dominant consideration. Here our goal should be to persuade such people to support policies which might appear, on the surface, to run counter to that self-interest but which in the long run make more sense.

Public attitudes toward criminals are a good area to in which to explore the conflict between short-term and long-term self-interest. Many voters are convinced that their own welfare and that of their families is best served by being "tough on crime" – by advocating the death penalty, mandatory sentences, "three strikes and you're out," the diminished use of probation and parole, the elimination of educational and recreational programs in prisons and the continuing exclusion of ex-criminals from the political process. Putting aside the question of whether these policies are really effective, even in the short run, it is increasingly clear that they entail some very substantial long-term costs, including the cost of building and operating a prison system which now houses nearly two million Americans as well as making many of those prisoners unfit to return to normal life. I suggest that drawing attention to these costs is more likely to persuade Americans to re-examine their support for all forms of "getting tough on crime" than any appeal to religious or humanitarian values. Similar analyses could be made in other areas of public policy.

Finally, we need to take very seriously those limitations, constitutional and otherwise, on the power of governments, corporations, and individuals to pursue their self-regarding objectives to the bitter end. The Supreme Court, in several recent opinions, has used the metaphor of hydraulic pressure to describe the tendency of all power to expand until checked by a superior force. The constitutional scheme which the founding fathers put in place contained three quite distinct limitations on the exercise of public power: the Bill of Rights, and related guarantees, which now protect citizens from abuses of public authority at all levels of government; a federal system which preserves the states as bulwarks against the abuse of national power; and a national government which is structured so as to divide power among its three branches. It is sometimes suggested that these limitations, especially those associated with a federal system, have become obsolete owing both to changes in our society and in our constitutional framework over the past 200+ years. That is, in my judgment, a profoundly erroneous view. I don't always agree with recent decisions of the Supreme Court striking down various exercises of Congressional power as beyond the scope of national power under the interstate commerce clause, but I am glad we have a Supreme Court that takes these limitations seriously.

Liberals are inclined to underestimate the capacity for the abuse of public power; conservatives are equally blind to the capacity for the abuse of private power. As we enter the 21st century we must be aware of both. On the one hand, the Bush Administration appears willing to use the catastrophe of September 11, 2001 and the hunt for terrorists as an excuse for subverting various constitutional guarantees; on the other hand recent scandals involving executive compensation, under-funded pensions, fraudulent stock trading, and attempts to evade U.S. regulations by moving operations "offshore" suggest that the private economy is not immune to the lure of money and the power it can buy. We must be vigilant against abuses of both private and public power.

If self-interest is ubiquitous, so is the need to compromise which lies at the heart of democratic politics. On more than one occasion one of my constituents has said, "What's right is right." The difficulty with this formulation of the standards that ought to govern conduct in public life is that it offers no guidance to the public official facing a choice between two kinds of rightness. Democracy is a good, but not one that should trump all others. The initiative, referendum, and recall are advocated as the ultimate expression of democratic values – "Let the people decide" – but as recent experience in California and Oregon demonstrates, they can wreak havoc with state budgets and the efficiency of state operations – and these, too, are important values. The same is true about electing judges, a practice defended as democratic, but one which collides with another important principle – fairness, which I think in this situation ought to trump democratic values.

Some years ago I was persuaded, against my better judgment, to address a conclave of Lutheran pastors on the topic, "Religion and Politics." In the question period that followed one elderly cleric put the question this way: "How can you put up with all those degrading compromises they are always making in Harrisburg?" I started to give a reply couched in more or less theoretical terms, then thought better of it. "Sir," I said in reply, "haven't you, as a clergyman, ever faced a situation where the Men's Bible Class has accumulated $2000 in their treasury which they want to spend re-surfacing the bowling alleys in the church annex. For you, on the other hand, helping combat AIDS in Africa is a much more compelling cause.

And so, in the end, you compromise, agreeing to spend $1000 on the bowling alleys and $1000 on AIDS." My questioner was not satisfied, but from the nods and chuckles I gathered that most of my listeners had got the point.

But compromise is difficult if you live in a universe where all questions are, at the bottom, moral questions. Among our presidents, Woodrow Wilson perhaps best exemplifies this cast of mind; it greatly complicated, and ultimately defeated, his attempt to persuade the Senate to ratify the League of Nations Treaty.

The question then arises, is nothing sacred, i.e., are there no principles of such transcendent importance that they should never be bargained away? The answer is more complex than most of my fellow citizens think.

As a Quaker I have always been opposed to capital punishment, believing that in addition to being expensive and ineffective it degrades the society which has frequent recourse to it. Suppose as a member of the Pennsylvania House I introduce a bill to outlaw capital punishment after a certain date. It is clear that I have no more than 50 of the 102 votes needed to pass the bill. One of my colleagues offers an amendment to impose a two-year moratorium on executions pending the report of a special commission appointed to study the whole issue. Do I support the amendment? Of course; it will buy us two years – and, if the commision's report is favorable, some powerful ammunition for eventually achieving abolition. All or nothing is as destructive in politics as it is in marriage.

A classic case of the best being enemy of the good occurred during the Nixon Administration. Prodded by Moynihan and others, Nixon proposed a system of family allowances, much like those employed by several European countries, to take the place of our much-maligned welfare system. It was scuttled by an unholy alliance of conservative Republicans who were against the whole idea and liberal Democrats who thought the allowances insufficiently generous. So welfare reform got postponed for 20 years, and when it took place assumed a much less benign form.

I was also wrong about what qualities are essential to success in public life. Given my background, it is not surprising that at 28 I had a somewhat elitist view of politics, overestimating the role of brain power and formal education and underestimating the role of experience and common sense in public life. In teaching American Government at Franklin and Marshall College during the 1960s I used to give what I called my "chastity quiz" – ten true/false statements designed to probe my students' understanding of the nature of democratic politics (the quiz itself was an early victim of coeducation and political correctness). One of my statements was, "in voting for candidates for public office you should generally prefer the candidate with the most impressive educational credentials." In my book this statement was false (as were the other nine). Whoever racked up the highest number of "Trues" was awarded the chastity belt to protect his innocence when venturing into the murky waters of American politics.

I can best illustrate this point by describing the career of Ernest P. Kline, Lieutenant Governor in the Shapp Administration. Ernie was raised in a working class neighborhood in Beaver County, just north of Pittsburgh. His father died when he was twelve. He never got beyond high school, but brains and a mellifluous voice won him rapid promotion from disc jockey to sportscaster to news announcer. At thirty he was appointed by Governor Lawrence to the position of workers' compensation referee, a position he filled with distinction. Then came election to the State Senate at thirty-six, elevation to Minority Leader and victory as Lieutenant Governor in 1970.

Ernie was a crucial member of the Shapp team, bringing to his work the knowledge, so indispensable, of "where the bodies are buried." Though not a reformer by instinct, he carried the ball for the administration in the Senate and was loyal to the Governor. And all this on a high school diploma! It was a tragedy for him and the Democratic party that by 1978 the Shapp Administration had worn out its welcome, and in the gubernatorial primary of that year Kline finished a distant third behind Flaherty and Casey. That was his "last hurrah" in the public arena which he had graced with singular lustre.

Not surprisingly my earlier view, that people who disagreed with me were either knaves or fools, also had to yield to a less judgmental outlook. I have encountered very few people in public life who were without scruple, people who again and again put their own welfare ahead of the public good. I have always suspected that the proportion of miscreants in politics is no higher than the proportion in the corporate world, a judgment fortified by recent corporate scandals. As for fools, i.e., those who can't evaluate evidence or reason from accepted premises, they are everywhere, but not peculiar to politics.

The truth of the matter is that most people who disagree with me do so not from base motives or stupidity, but simply because they bring to public life a set of preconceptions that are different from my own. Moreover, this is a liberating, not a confining discovery; it is much easier to deal persuasively with your colleagues if you start from the premise that they are simply mistaken rather than knaves or fools.

Believing as I once did that politics – government, anyway – required only that we define problems, amass evidence about them, identify alternative solutions and then select and carry out the one that seems most likely to address the problem, it was natural to conclude that most public problems could in some sense be "solved," much as a mathematician solves an equation. But a number of factors make the solution of many public questions far more difficult than even the most abstruse mathematical equation.

1. We don't all begin from the same premises. As I write the issue which most divides Americans nationally is the legitimate scope of governmental action. Free marketers on the right – followers of Milton Friedman – would confine the national government largely to defense and civil order, while ultra liberals on the left would allow just about any government activity that did not infringe on liberties protected by the Bill

of Rights. The vast majority of Americans being center right or center left subscribe to neither dogma. But if we can't agree on whether government should take action at all then agreement on what action to take is obviously remote.

2. We may agree that a problem exists but define it in ways that make solutions difficult. Senator Moynihan points out, for example, that as long as the problem of death and injury from auto accidents was seen in terms of the need to alter the behavior of motorists, it was intractable; only when investigators broadened their field of inquiry to include auto design did we began to make real progress.

3. The evidence about what will work may be contradictory or inconclusive. Studies that attempt to evaluate the effectiveness of school vouchers or charter schools point in several directions, none of them very helpful to the lawmaker.

4. Even where there is consensus about the best remedy, we may not be able or willing to devote the resources required to make a real difference. In the case of drug abuse, for example, few states have been willing to fund the kind of intensive counseling and therapeutic programs that might lead to major changes in behavior.

5. In a democratic society elections bring about changes in the relevant players, making it hard to apply policies consistently over a long period of time. In Mifflin County, a majority

favoring school consolidation became, overnight, a majority pledged to block consolidation.

In spite of these difficulties candidates for public office continue to make pronouncements like the one in Governor Shapp's inaugural to the effect that "no problem is so great that we cannot surmount it." If these pronouncements were cost-free, we could dismiss them as mere puffery, calculated to inspire the hearer with a sense of the speaker's courage and pertinacity. But they are not cost-free; the price of making these exaggerated claims for the effectiveness of governmental policies is cynicism on the part of the electorate, a conviction that politicians will say anything in order to get elected. And that is a high price to pay.

These difficulties call into question my youthful confidence in "progress," the notion that we are moving inexorably toward an ideal form of democratic capitalism in which Americans generally will be better educated, healthier, better off, and therefore happier than their parents and grandparents. Progress is possible, but it is by no means inevitable. Scientific research will continue to provide the impetus for advances in medicine, communications, transportation and many other fields; whether we can create the political conditions under which these gains can be widely shared is an open question.

I return at the end to the question of why so many of my fellow citizens are apathetic or cynical about public life. It has something to do, I think, with the Puritan culture which emigrated to these shores. That culture was strengthened by the conditions of frontier life, although why it should persist more than a century after Frederick

Jackson Turner proclaimed the end of the frontier is something of a mystery. Senator Moynihan has suggested that there is a "Protestant tendency to be dissatisfied with what might be called normal human behavior." Beginning with exaggerated expectations we lapse into indifference or hostility when those expectations are not fulfilled.

So I have shed or modified many of the assumptions with which I began a political life forty-five years ago. But a disillusioned idealist can go in one of two directions. He can become a cynic, concluding that people are motivated solely by self-interest, and that progress is itself an illusion. Or he can embrace what I have earlier called a "pragmatic" theory of politics. (I don't use the word "realist" because it implies a too-ready acceptance of things as they are.) Jack Kennedy once called himself an "idealist without illusions." That more accurately describes my own mindset. I haven't abandoned the effort to make the world a little better place, but I have discovered that it's a hell of a lot harder that I thought it would be.

So I have rejected cynicism, an easy choice; but I have also rejected ideology and the certitude that springs from ideology. I am with Learned Hand, when he says that "the spirit of liberty is the spirit that is not quite sure that it is right." And with Disraeli, who is supposed to have said, "I wish I were as sure of anything as Lord Morley is of everything." My intellectual heroes are, on this side of the Atlantic Oliver Wendell Holmes, Jr., and Daniel Patrick Moynihan, and on the other side George Orwell and Winston Churchill: Holmes, because he refused to write his own prejudices into the Constitution; Moynihan, because he understood that progress in a democratic polity is messy and incremental at best; Churchill, because he didn't let consistency prevail over larger considerations; and Orwell, because he came eventually to understand that fanaticism on the left was as threatening to democratic values as fanaticism on the right.

Have I been successful in reeducating myself? Not entirely. I am reminded of the words with which young Mario describes his cousin Oliver Alden in the prologue to Santayana's only novel, "The Last Puritan." Oliver, says Mario, is a "Puritan, who decided on Puritan grounds that Puritanism was a bad thing – and went right on being one." That isn't a bad description of my own fate; I am an idealist who decided on pragmatic grounds that idealism in its purest form was a mistake but was unable to shed all of my illusions. Perhaps that is not, after all, a bad thing; my tempered idealism is what gives me the energy to persevere in the face of what otherwise might seem overwhelming odds.

Index

About The Author

John C. Pittenger was born in Philadelphia, Pa in 1930 and was educated in the public schools of Swarthmore, Pa and at the Phillips Exeter Academy, Harvard College and Harvard Law School. He served in the United States Army from 1952 to 1955.

In 1958 Pittenger settled in Lancaster, Pa where he practiced law for the next seven years. He first ran for the state House of Representatives in 1962, beginning the career in local and state politics which furnishes the subject matter of this book.

In addition to his political activities Pittenger has been a college teacher, a law school dean and professor, a squash coach, a farmer and an author (The Pursuit of Justice, with Henry Bragdon, Macmillan, 1966). He was awarded an honorary degree by Franklin and Marshall College in 1981. Pittenger is married to the former Pauline Leet.